AMERICAN SUNSHINE

Rays of Hope and Opportunity

By
JAY LUCAS

American Sunshine
©2018 Jay Lucas
New Hampshire

Publisher
Elite Online Publishing
63 East 11400 South #230
Sandy, UT 84070
www.EliteOnlinePublishing.com

ISBN: 978-1986535724

FOREWORD

American Sunshine is a positive, uplifting and refreshing book. In contrast to so many contemporary voices that shout that America is on the brink of disaster, this book looks at historic American reality; a reality built upon timeless core principles and based in the time proven results found in positive belief.

This is an area very familiar to me. For many years, I was the chief lieutenant to Dr. Norman Vincent Peale, the author of *The Power of Positive Thinking*. Dr. Peale was an inspirational leader and tireless proponent of the concept that positive thinkers create positive results. In fact, he is noted for saying that whether you believe you can or whether you believe you can't – you are right.

I see Dr. Peale's underlying philosophy throughout this book. But I see much more, too. Dr. Peale believed his book started a great conversation. He encouraged me to write a book about *The Power BEHIND Positive Thinking*. Jay Lucas has done a terrific job of expanding once again to reveal *The Power BEYOND Positive Thinking*; especially as he illuminates how those fundamental principles apply to achieving a positive future for our great country.

He describes the underlying values that lie at the core of the American spirit. He explains how these values have helped us through our history and then reveals how they can overcome any challenge we face as we move this great country forward.

At the same time, there is certain lightness and sense of humor on display throughout the book. I love the way that the illustrations in each chapter capture the essence of the message that Jay communicates so well. And, they do so in a clear-eyed yet fun, good-spirited way.

This truly is an important and thoughtful book. I hope you enjoy reading it as much as I have. I also hope that you will embrace the lessons in the book and renew your positive belief in yourself, in your community and your faith in our great country.

Eric Fellman

ACKNOWLEDGEMENTS

Writing this book has been an enormously energizing experience. It has also been incredibly humbling. The process of clarifying my thoughts and attempting to articulate my core beliefs has made me realize how important the contributions of others have been in shaping my vision and values.

I am deeply thankful to have grown up in a wonderful small town with incredible parents. I am also thankful to have had grandparents who gave me a sense of history as I listened to their stories about what life had been like years ago. And, in all of this, emerged a deep appreciation and respect for the core values that have shaped America. And, likewise, a 'Can Do' optimism that is such a vital part of the American spirit.

I cannot overstate the importance of these early experiences in providing a foundation for the thoughts, stories and beliefs that are sprinkled throughout the book.

Meanwhile, the actual writing of the book has been very much a team effort. Great thanks go to my editor, Kate Frank, who has done a superb job of sharpening the final product and who has been such fun to work with. The same is true for my publishers at Elite Online Publishing led by Melanie Johnson and Jenn Foster. They are true professionals running a great organization.

Very importantly, I give a great deal of credit to Jane Hanson and Sandy Chase who sparked the inspiration to push forward with this book and who demonstrated great patience as we recorded these chapters in multiple sessions at odd times, spanning weekends and evenings over many months. They were great coaches and wonderful friends; very creative, thoughtful and talented.

Great thanks to Eric Fellman for contributing a superbly crafted Foreword. Eric had the pleasure of working directly with Dr. Norman Vincent Peale for a number of years and inevitably exudes the optimism and enthusiastic spirit best articulated in Dr. Peale's inspirational work, 'The Power of Positive Thinking.' Well done and appreciated, Eric.

And, my brother Sky is the absolute best; a keen intellect with a wry sense of humor. Not to mention, as you enjoy some of the great illustrations and cartoons in the book, we have Sky to thank. He introduced me to Sam Keiser. Sam produced the illustrations for Sky's book and was kind enough to help me as well. Sam's cartoons help liven up the book in a fun way. And, if you look closely, you will see that his illustrations inject subtle humor while also emphasizing the primary message of each chapter in a uniquely visual format. Thank you, Sam.

A special thank you as well to Ryan Knowles, B.J. Perry and Ross Berry who have helped in so many ways, especially with regard to the branding and 'look and feel' of the book as well as our digital media.

Then, last and most important, my family; first and foremost, my wonderful Karen; none of this would be possible without her. And, to all of our children who contribute in so many wonderful ways; Lincoln, Morgan, Gates, Ryan, Ian, Erin and Justin.

Heartfelt thanks and greatly appreciated.

INTRODUCTION

American Sunshine paints an optimistic view of our future. It is all about the 'Can Do' spirit – and what can be 'achieved' if you really and whole heartedly 'believe.'

The first section, 'Positive Rays That Bind Us Together,' identifies areas of common ground - ranging from a chapter on dogs to an essay on millennials. In addition, there is a chapter outlining a point of view on sports, as well some thoughts one of my favorite sports teams, the Boston Red Sox. It describes the positive spirit and eternal hope of the loyal sports fan, no matter what team you love and support. More than we realize, we share common sentiments and experiences and these ties serve to unite us in a uniquely positive way.

The next section, 'The Power of Belief' describes the enormous impact of positive energy, faith and ultimately belief. In other words, it demonstrates the maxim – if you believe, you can achieve. Included are real life examples of people who have accomplished amazing feats that would have been impossible if not for their unwavering belief. Our beliefs truly do determine our destiny.

The third pillar in the philosophy of American Sunshine builds on the 'Positive Rays' and 'The Power of Belief' and attempts to explain the essence of 'The American Spirit.' In other words, it articulates what is so truly special about our great country. It identifies the key elements that lie at the core of American exceptionalism and celebrates our 'Can Do' spirit and sense of continual optimism.

With these pillars firmly in place, the next task is to understand their relationship and application to our current situation. Therefore, this section tackles such important issues as Education, Immigration and even Freedom of Speech in America today. It articulates a belief that we can transcend old, tired approaches with a spirit of innovation, creativity and positive belief in ourselves. It emphasizes the importance of reaffirming our core values and building upon our strengths.

Lastly, the question then becomes how we can put these principles into practice in our local communities and in our everyday lives. There are examples of how we are actually doing so and thereby having a positive impact on behalf of numerous deserving individuals, including our veterans, our children, our towns, women in developing countries and more.

TABLE OF CONTENTS

SECTION ONE

POSITIVE RAYS THAT
BIND US TOGETHER

CHAPTER ONE

DOGS
A POSITIVE CONVERSATION

Anyone who has had a dog in his or her life will tell you dogs embody a natural positive energy. Sometimes I think if everybody in America had a dog, it would be a wonderful thing, especially for our kids and our seniors... I love dogs. Dog lovers can enjoy the pleasure of something other people may never know.

Here are a few of their most positive qualities:

- They're loyal
- They're very selfless
- They're friendly
- And every time they wag their tail, positive energy radiates out to us

Sparky – My Best Friend

My favorite dog of all time was named Sparky. He was also my best friend. Sparky and I were together almost 14 years. He was a little black dog we got from the animal shelter. He was an overweight mutt, but he was the friendliest, nicest dog ever, at least as far as I was concerned...

If any dog was ever loyal, it was Sparky. I used to go out for runs with him. The poor little guy was not an athlete. He would trail behind me. After a couple of miles, I'd look back and he'd be several hundreds of yards behind me. He would be running in a strange, funny diagonal way with his tongue hanging out. He was doing the absolute best he could because he wanted to stick right by my side.

I also remember a time when I was going through a very difficult business situation. It had been an awful day at work. I came home, only to open the door and find Sparky waiting. He loved me. He was loyal. He didn't care what happened to me at the office. Really, within seconds, my whole day changed. My attitude turned around in an instant. It's just wonderful what a dog can do to lift your spirits.

Lessons in Loyalty

It may be a truism to refer to dogs as loyal, but I do think of loyalty every time I think of dogs.

Sparky was fiercely loyal

Sparky was fiercely loyal. Dogs are fiercely loyal.

There was a time during my life when I was traveling a lot. I would leave on Monday and come back on Friday. And, I was doing this week after week. Happily, every single Friday when I came back, there was Sparky right at the front door looking out the window – waiting for me loyally. Dogs never ask: "Where were you?" "What were you doing?"

I wondered how Sparky knew exactly when I was coming home on Fridays. So, I decided to ask my daughter, Morgan. I said, "Morgan, it's uncanny. Sparky is right there the moment I come home. It's amazing that he knows or senses exactly when I'll be coming home. How does that happen?"

She said, "Dad, I don't think you understand. When you leave on Monday, Sparky gets right by that door, looking out the window. He stays there and waits for you the whole week while you're gone."

Now – that's loyalty!

Famous Dogs in History

Sometimes I think of our presidents and the first families. I think about the crises they go through and the issues they have to confront. I think about the dogs in the White

House and how they must perk up some of our nation's leaders.

You may remember:

- Ronald and Nancy Reagan had Rex
- The Obamas had Bo and Sonny
- The senior Bushes had the cute little beagle named Millie

Visiting Dogs for Recovery

...having the companionship of a dog can make a real difference...

The same positive spirit found in Sparky and the White House dogs makes dogs great visitors to our hospitals. If you've been in a hospital recently you most likely may have seen a dog, or several dogs, walking with their handlers from room to room cheering up patients. You just have to believe these dogs must have a positive effect on the patients and their recoveries.

Dogs are also companions to our veterans who return with PTSD. It's been proven that having the companionship of a dog can make a real difference in creating a sustainable and stable source of comfort. The dogs can be extremely important in a veteran's return and transition back into civilian life.

Obvious Value of Dogs

You know, it's pretty obvious, isn't it? If we could all have a dog – or better yet – if we could all behave a little bit more like dogs, this world would clearly be a better place.

CHAPTER TWO

SPORTS

I've been involved in sports for as early as I can remember. And, it's been a terrifically positive experience. I can remember growing up in Newport, New Hampshire, right across from the Newport Town Common, where we played pickup games of baseball with my younger brother and our friends. What great fun. Playing Little League Baseball and High School football down the hill...All of these were such formative experiences in growth and development. Being involved in sports for me has been a way of life as well as a great way to learn how to work with others; develop self-discipline and so many other good things.

Sports and the Value of Teamwork

You know, in sports you set a goal. You work hard each day. You measure your progress as you get better, and better, and better. You do this both on an individual basis and importantly, also as a team. It is better for you than you might think...

When working together as a team, it's not primarily about your role as an individual. In fact, most often, it's just the opposite. It's about subordinating your personal interest to the interests of the team.

One of the best examples of selfless 'teamwork' would be the Boston Celtics of the 1960s and 1970s. During that period, there were teams with better athletes and better superstars, but the Boston Celtics exemplified what it means to play as a team. The leader of the team, and the personification of this mentality, was their center Bill Russell. A gifted athlete...Small for the position by some standards, only six feet, nine inches... – but more important, a focused competitor, thoroughly dedicated to teamwork and team achievement. As a result, the Boston Celtics of the 'Bill Russell

Era' achieved unparalleled success. During Russell's 13 seasons as a Boston Celtic, the team won 11 World Championships. Talk about planning ahead? Bill Russell was a great rebounder...Bill was quoted as saying: "I got a lot of rebounds yes, but I got most of my rebounds before they took a shot." Positioning, thinking, yes, thinking like a true team player2026

Eleven championships in thirteen seasons. Absolutely amazing. And, keep in mind they were continually going up against the most dominant individual player of the entire era, Wilt Chamberlain. Chamberlain was essentially a 'scoring machine,' even tallying 100 points in a single game. Yet, the Celtics won championships year after year with selfless teamwork.

Adversity

At the same time, when engaging in sports there is inevitably the experience of losing. This of course is never the hoped for result – but nonetheless provides valuable learning. You do run into failures. You hit barriers sometimes. You need to learn how to deal with it. And, of course, it's really important to learn how to take the adversity, push through it and convert it to a positive outcome.

Three Troubling Trends in Sports

We, as a nation, love sports; and while I am tremendously bullish and positive about sport in America, there are several trends today that do trouble me. When I was growing up, we would play all of the sports according to the

I think kids lose something by not being able to have the general experience of being a kid, playing a sport, and having fun.

13

season. In the fall, we'd play football or soccer. In the winter, it would be basketball. In the springtime, we would break out the baseball equipment, along with all the other things you could do when the weather warmed up. New glove? New shoes? New bat? Exciting!!!

ONE: Specialization Too Early

However, today I see something quite different. Namely, pressure on kids to specialize in a particular sport and do the specializing on an exclusive basis. They get pushed pretty hard. At 11 or 12, they may get placed on a travel team. Maybe it's baseball, or maybe it's soccer. Whatever it might be, I think kids lose something by not being able to have the general experience of being a kid, playing multiple sports, and having fun.

TWO: Participation Trophies

Another troubling trend is the idea of 'participation trophies.' You know, in sports, there are winners and losers. We want to encourage people to really work their hardest, have them understand what it takes to be a winner and to be rewarded for that great effort. When they truly earn a gold medal, we want them to internalize the message "Hey, I earned this reward through my effort, my persistence and sometimes through my courage." When everyone is equally being awarded a 'participation trophy,' excellence in effort and in result is not being properly recognized.

THREE: Deemphasizing Sports

I have noticed the beginnings of a trend among some to deemphasize sports and to minimize the role of sports in our society. This is most pronounced in some areas of academia including a number of our leading colleges. I stand squarely on the opposite side of this trend. Sports can play such an important role in developing self-discipline and stimulating active engagement and physical fitness, we cannot let this happen.

Reason for Optimism

Nonetheless, despite these ripples, as we look out on America, we should optimistic about the positive role sports will continue to play in our society. We see all those moms and dads going to games, participating as Little League coaches, and getting up at 4 or 5 in the morning to take their son or daughter to the swimming pool or hockey practice. We need to be teaching our youth the value of competition, how to be good sports and how to work with each other collaboratively as teammates toward a common goal – these are all such important tasks. And, central to our fabric as a nation.

CHAPTER THREE

RUNNING

Running is a sport, but it's also a passion. Although other people have passions to help reduce stress and create physical fitness, running is the activity I enjoy.

Running is something I have done since I graduated from high school many years ago. I love running. It has so many great benefits. It's good for you physically; it gives you time to think; you get outdoors; get to see neighborhoods and places you might not otherwise get to enjoy. I can go on and on. The boredom factor does not exist for me...It may be an inhibiting factor for others...But it is in an odd way, "my quiet time"

At the same time, I have to confess, while I truly am a very enthusiastic runner, I will never be setting any world records. But, I've done some marathons (which by the way can be quite painful if you have not fully trained – or if you go out too fast – i.e. me, Boston, 2006 – uggh!) But, it's a great sport almost anyone can pick up, at almost any age. You can set goals for yourself and you can make it fun.

The Physical Benefits of Running

Running has great health benefits. Your heart, lungs, and legs all benefit from a daily running routine. Running really benefits nearly every part of your body.

In fact, studies have shown that cardiovascular health is greatly improved through running. It can increase HDL levels, helps on overall cholesterol, can prevent obesity and type 2 diabetes; can reduce heart disease, high blood pressure, stroke and some cancers. It can also give your immune system an important boost through an increase in white blood cells. Good stuff all around.

And, what I also enjoy, maybe even more than the physical benefits, are the mental benefits. It just makes you feel good. You get a chance to get off by yourself, clear your head from the day's activities, think good thoughts and get a total mental re-fresh.

The Running Discipline

Part of the running habit is also the self-discipline. If you get up every day and run in the mornings, it sets your day and is a really good way of saying, "Hey, I've accomplished something."

Running is a terrific way to clear your mind and think.

Running is a terrific way to clear your mind and think. "I'm out there by myself. I don't have a phone. No emails, no texting, nothing to bother me." Our mind just gets into a different place. Thoughts just pop into the brain in really good ways. Thoughts we never think about during the course of a normal day.

Running to Explore

Beyond the physical and mental benefits, running is a great way to explore. In my business I tend to travel quite a bit and often find myself getting into a city very late in the evening. My business associates or colleagues may want to meet the next day at breakfast or schedule an early morning meeting, and that's fine – but I have an even earlier plan. I get up super early to sneak in a run and go out to explore. I see interesting parts of the city and have a fresh, exciting adventure along the way. Plus, I show up at the meeting feeling better, more alert and probably happier than anyone else in attendance.

Lately, I have been running a lot in New York City. It surprises people to learn I run on the streets, rather than on the pathways by the water or in Central Park. It's really fun. Imagine running in New York City and coming down to a streetlight, not knowing which way you're going to be able to go. The streetlight will be red or green. Maybe you go through or maybe you have to dart to the right, or to the left? By the time I am two or three miles into this, I'm off in a different place, a place that I never could have planned to be, with all the spontaneous lefts and rights along the way - not being able to predict the lights in advance – red or green.

Running as a Bonding Experience

For me, morning runs are the best... but from time to time, I have been able to enjoy going for family runs mostly during the day.... All of my kids, now young adults, have varying degrees of enthusiasm towards running. It is a fun activity we enjoy together as a family.

We have also made the annual "Turkey Trot" each Thanksgiving into a fun family tradition. We sign up for a race on Thanksgiving morning – and run a race, usually with hundreds of other running enthusiasts, as well as quite a few 'once a year' runners. There's something about the experience that makes the family Thanksgiving feel special. Plus, it really makes you feel like you deserve a great turkey dinner later that afternoon.

Another family running tradition is a little bit more serious. It's a half marathon, a 13.1 mile run in Lowell, Massachusetts called the Bay State. The run takes place just around the same time as my birthday every year in mid to late October. All of my children have run it together with me at various times.

The fall foliage is awesome. It builds family bonding, is a really a great experience together and is something we just absolutely love to do. Plus the race is a 'runner's dream' – a totally flat course on cool fall day – so you have a great opportunity to run a super-fast race – and impress yourself with your time – all the while knowing it's probably a bit artificial, given the near 'perfect' conditions.

The Pitfalls of Running

I have talked mostly about the benefits of running, but there are some pitfalls. One such pitfall is an unexpected dog along your route. Some people fear dogs, but I have never let them bother me. My strategy is based on the fact I'm bigger than a dog. In my experience, on the few occasions when I have been confronted, I have found if you can strike a little bit of fear into the heart of the dog, typically they'll back off. (Thankfully, although I'm not one hundred percent sure what may happen on the day that I finally meet the dog that doesn't back off. More on this later, if it ever happens.)

I did have an encounter with a bull once. Based on personal experience, I know, however, I know that bulls, (and bears for that matter) are a different story, as I did once have a face-to-face encounter with a bull. I was in Spain on vacation with my family, and we were staying at a resort. I snuck away for a run during the middle of the day. There was a rural road leading up to a mountain nearby and it looked like a good place for run. So, I headed on up. The further up I got, the more rural it became. I began see farm animals in the fields on the side of the road.

When I got far enough up, suddenly, I came upon a bull in the middle of my path, staring right at me. He was only about 30 feet away. I don't know very much about bulls but I do know that they can be very mean. And, this particular bull did not give me any reason to *It's important to have these positive opportunities to get physically active, invest in your health and well-being.* question the stereotype. Moreover, the way he was staring at me and lowering his head – made it pretty clear he did not want me running up his road.

I started to back away slowly. He started walking toward me. I started backing away faster and he started walking faster. I decided to run for my life. As I was running down the hill I remember being very scared. In fact, I became even more frightened when I noticed there were sharp rock cliff formations on each side of the road – essentially forming twenty-foot walls on both sides. There was no escape. I couldn't dart into the woods or do some other tricky thing to evade the bull. I just had to run. I ran as far as I could, and as fast as I could, until I finally I dared look behind me. He wasn't there. I thought "Oh my God. I know I've never run so fast in all my life."

Running is a Great Passion

Despite the occasional dog, and the once in a lifetime (hopefully) bull, running or working out should be a wonderful part of our life. The physical, mental and even family and social benefits can be enormous.

While running is my passion, I also know other people have their own unique pursuits and passions that can be equally strong and beneficial. Some people like cycling. Some people like gardening. And, some like just getting into the outdoors, fishing, hunting, hiking, whatever. It's important to have these positive opportunities to get physically active, invest in your health and well being

So, no matter what type of activity you enjoy most and fits best with your interests and lifestyle, I encourage you to participate – and to do so with vigor, joy and enthusiasm. It's great for the body and for your mind. And, undoubtedly, the activity will make you a more positive contributor to all of those around you.

CHAPTER FOUR

BOSTON RED SOX

This chapter is about the Boston Red Sox. It's about Red Sox Nation and the deep passionate feeling we in New England have for our team. But it's also about the joys and sorrows of being a true blue fan of whatever team has captured your heart. Let me explain.

Growing up in New Hampshire, in New England, it's in the water. It's in the blood. You're going to be a Red Sox fan. It's just one of those things. It's definitely going to happen. It's a feeling and an experience that is uniquely New England. It's different from just being a sports fan. In fact, it's very close to being a religion. It's one of the most important things that binds us together as New Englanders. We really love our Boston Red Sox.

For people outside New England, it is difficult to appreciate how pervasive the passion for the Red Sox throughout every town and city in the region. ...No matter which shop you go into to get a cup of coffee or a newspaper anywhere in New England and you ask the cashier; "How did they do last night? He or she will say they won or lost and report the score...Who is they? They are the Boston Red Sox...Pure and simple...All unspoken but all known...

Shared Suffering

Part of the reason we are such a tight-knit group is that we have a long, rich history of suffering together. During all those years when I was

I have vivid memories. Oh, my goodness gracious, it was suffering.

growing up, we were continually losing. Did I just say we? Yes it was "we" And we were really suffering in a common sort of agony. It's all part of our ethos. Part of being a Red Sox fan.

We have vivid memories. Oh, my goodness gracious, it was suffering. It was so hard. Even as a little boy growing up and following the Boston Red Sox. My mother and father were huge fans as well. They were thoroughly devoted.

They both lived a long life yet never to see a World Series victory...

Now, keep in mind, the Red Sox had not won the World Series since 1918. Both my parents were born after that. So, during their entire lifetime the Red Sox had never won a World Series. They had come close on a number of occasions...which is almost worse than not being in contention at all. In fact, on second thought, coming close is decidedly worse.

Tradition of Coming Close

And, the tradition of coming close – only to lose in the end – is deep in the psyche of the Red Sox Nation. Older Red Sox fans speak painfully about 1946 – when the Red Sox finally made it to the World Series. But, of course, in the seventh game they lost. And, shortly thereafter, in 1949, lost the pennant in a final playoff game to the New York Yankees.

Then in 1967, we came ever so close once again. It was the season known to Red Sox fans as the Impossible Dream. There was Carl Yastrzemski and Jim Lonborg. And, Rico Petrocelli catching a shallow pop fly to shortstop to clinch the American League Pennant. Then, consistent with tradition, we suffered a painful loss to the St. Louis Cardinals in the seventh game of the World Series. Bob Gibson...Drat!

That was a really tough one. And, it stayed with us. But in another way, it gave us renewed hope. For a whole new generation of Red Sox fans, we knew we could come close.

We didn't know if we could win, but our hopes were being renewed.

And, yes, in the 1970's we had some great teams with Jim Rice, Carlton Fisk, Freddie Lynn and Luis Tiant, among others. But, the painful tradition of coming close so many times continued. The true agony of losing the 1975 World Series. Especially after the dramatic comeback in Game Six. If you're a Red Sox fan, you really remember these things. Awful moments.

Then, the terrible 1978 playoff game against the New York Yankees, when Bucky *^##*^ Dent hit the home run. It crushed us...absolutely crushed us. And, of course, it pains us to even talk about 1986 and the New York Mets. When, near the end of Game Six, it flashed up on the screen, near the apparent end of the game: "Congratulations – World Champions - Boston Red Sox." Then, to subsequently lose the game, and the Series. Uggh. It was just so devastating.

Take Him OUT!

Nearly as bad was 2003, when it seemed that our beloved Red Sox were destined to finally win. We had a really terrific team – and our ace pitcher Pedro Martinez seemed unbeatable. We had made it all the way to the American League Championship Series and were playing a final game against our bitter rival, the New York Yankees. Pedro was on the mound, the Red Sox were winning and it was late in the game, in the eighth inning. It finally appeared we were on our way.

But there was one catch. Everyone in New England knew that Pedro could only throw 90 pitches or so in a game before getting tired. Everyone in New England knew it was time to take him out.

It was right about that time that Red Sox manager, Grady Little, went out to the mound. It was silent throughout New England. It was a cold, sort of crisp fall evening. It was dark and there was this eerie silence. You could feel and almost hear everyone in New England saying in unison "Take him out. Take him out."

And, of course, consistent with Red Sox tradition up to that point, he inexplicably left him in. The Yankees rallied and we ended up losing the game. And, it was really a disaster... I remember going into the Panera the next morning and experiencing an eerie somber silence. An exhausted Red Sox Nation was horribly depressed.

Hope Springs Eternal

But, despite suffering such painful defeat, the wonderful thing about being a Red Sox fan - is that 'hope' truly does spring eternal. A tradition of defeats notwithstanding, we continued to 'Believe!' And, it was just then, in 2004, that our undying faith was about to be rewarded.

It was a moment of great intensity because it was absolutely clear Roberts had to steal second base for the Red Sox to have a meaningful chance of winning

In the fall of 2004, there came a moment... a magical moment. It was when the entire sweep of Red Sox history was magically reversed. The Red Sox were on the verge of being eliminated from the American League Championship – yet again by the New York Yankees. Then came the moment. When in the eighth inning, the Red Sox sent a pinch runner named Dave Roberts out to substitute for the runner on first base. It was a moment of great intensity because it was absolutely clear Roberts had to steal second base for the Red Sox to have a meaningful chance of winning.

The Yankees knew it. The Red Sox knew it. Everybody in the country watching the game knew it. They all knew he was going to be running down to try to steal second base as soon as the pitcher, Mariano Rivera, began delivering the pitch. About a three second run..."Here we go!" Nope...not yet...Three pick off moves to first base...Now, "Game on" It was just one of those moments.

As if almost in slow motion, as I recall. The wind up. The pitch. Roberts dashes for second base. Dives head first. And barely beats the tag, Derick Jeter upset...he thought he made the tag... Safe! Dave Roberts stole second base! A collective sigh of relief was felt throughout Red Sox Nation. But it was far more than that. It was if suddenly there was a confidence. A belief or faith that winning was actually possible. Perhaps even inevitable. It was the moment when the Red Sox fortunes dramatically turned around.

From that moment forward, the Red Sox rolled to one victory after another. Beating the Yankees in three consecutive games to win the pennant. They then summarily defeated the St. Louis Cardinals in the World Series, sweeping the Series in four games.

Strangely, during that entire run there was truly never a doubt. Dave Roberts stealing second base marked the instant, the moment when belief took on a life of its own.

Of course, following the victory, the first Red Sox world championship in eighty-six years, it was enormously exciting to be a New Englander. We were thrilled to be Red Sox fans and watch the parade in downtown Boston. The duck boats, everyone celebrating.

I must say I was sitting at home watching the duck boats and did well up with tears at one point, thinking of my parents. There was an article in our "Boston Globe" It was a quote that: "Who did you think about ...Who did you love? Wish they could have known" I thought about the fact that my parents had lived from 1921 and 1925, respectively, until both passing away in 2003, only to miss the 2004 season. Never during their lifetimes did they have the opportunity to watch their beloved Red Sox win the World Championship.

Hopefully, this gives a sense of what it's like to be a Red Sox fan.

Passion and Belief

In a larger sense, however, I share this story because being a Red Sox fan is more than just being someone who likes to watch baseball games and cheer for the home team. It is about both passion and belief. It is a positive outlet for emotional attachment. It provides a source of shared experience. We cherish the traditions of parents and grandparents taking their children to Fenway Park or whatever park...– and sharing them passing on - a true family experience.

And, of course, being a New Englander, the Red Sox are my team. But, I am sure that there a similar feelings and positive bonding experiences amongst fans of other teams and in other sports across our nation. Chicago has the beloved Cubbies. Wisconsin loves the Packers. Cleveland is nuts about the Cavaliers. And, I could go on.

The point is that it's positive and it's fun. It's one of those things that binds us together. And, as such, fan'dom is a rich part of the American tradition. It's a source of pride and passion.

CHAPTER FIVE

MILLENNIALS

Millennials receive an immense amount of criticism. They get criticized by both the popular press and society in general. I'm here to tell you it's undeserved.

Millennials are generally defined as the generation born in the 1980s and 1990s, and who came of age in the 21st century. I should know a bit about millennials because all of our children are millennials.

Millennials are Criticized

Criticism of millennials takes many forms. Here are several of the more prominent depictions. I suspect they may be quite familiar to you. Millennials are characterized as being 'glued to their phones.' They are constantly texting, while thoroughly lacking in such traditional communication skills as having direct conversations, either face to face, or ironically even over their phones.

They are also described as being thoroughly self-absorbed, self-focused and possessing a certain entitlement mentality. In other words, 'it's all about them.' The world owes them everything. Along these same lines in fact, the Urban Dictionary definition of millennials has even described them as 'precious little snowflakes.'

Well, I have a different view. While popular opinion may disagree, millennials deserve our well-deserved respect. They represent a great generation.

Some Perspective

To view millennials properly, you really need to develop an historical context. It is a truism that every generation looks at the one coming up

Millennials are going to reinvent the way we live, the way we work, the way we communicate, the way we organize our lives.

behind it with some degree of misgiving and often will be unduly critical. For instance, take the generation of the

1960s and 1970s. Baby boomers were characterized as hippies, protesters, and the 'Woodstock generation.' While undoubtedly there was truth to some of the characterization, these descriptions did not apply to all or even the vast majority of baby boomers. This is also true of the gross generalizations being applied to millennials.

To put all this in a more positive light, I think a better description for those coming of age in the '60's and '70's would be that they were the generation that challenged everything. Well, in a similar sense, I believe, millennials will come to be known as the generation that will reinvent everything. Millennials are going to reinvent the way we live, the way we work, the way we communicate, the way we organize our lives.

And, when you think about it, who could be in a better position to do this? This generation growing up in the '80's and '90's has had such a vastly different life experience than those who have come before them.

Unlike boomers, millenials while growing up had cell phones, and then eventually, smartphones, that became an integral part of their life experience. They were texting when they were three years old. Instead of going to the mall, their natural reflex is to order on Amazon and of course, expect almost immediate delivery.

While car ownership has been a source of pride for earlier generations, even a rite of passage, millennials have 'reinvented' the perception and status of car ownership. Large numbers of millennials choose not to own a car. Instead, they are into 'car sharing' or simply go to their phone, access Uber, and a ride shows up.

And, of course, they are 'reinventing' the 9-5, Monday thru Friday work schedule. They eschew the corporate career and instead fashion a very different work-life for themselves. They may not to go into the office or place of work at all, but instead work remotely. They think "Why do I need to go into the office if I can do my work from home - or from Starbucks of course?"

The Entrepreneur Generation

Given this radically different life experience, millennials find themselves in a wonderful position to reinvent the world. In fact, they are already well on their way to reinventing the world of business. Millennials are distinctly entrepreneurial and are successfully starting innovative businesses, many of which leverage information sources and technologies that were not even in existence for earlier generations. In fact, in a recent survey conducted by Bentley College, a full two-thirds of millennials (67%) indicated that it was their intent to start and own their own business.

This is particularly great news in that it has never been easier to start a business. Entrepreneurs can download the entire infrastructure and support system needed to start a business right from the cloud, including the accounting system, legal system, and logistical support. They can access global markets quickly and cost effectively via the internet. Capital has never been more available, especially for innovative business ideas.

As a result, millennials are starting businesses left and right, and not surprisingly, many of these new businesses are experiencing explosive growth. For instance, Airbnb was founded by a millennial. This peer-to-peer lodging service where you can list your apartment or house on the web and rent it out for short stays is thoroughly revolutionizing and reinventing the hotel and hospitality industry.

Another millennial founded business is. Chalk.com. Although not as well-known as Airbnb, I really do like what they are doing. Chalk.com is an app already being used in more than 20,000 classrooms around the country. The app allows teachers to be more productive, plan their lessons, and administer their classes.

I also love the story of Dosed.com. It demonstrates another very important theme so prevalent in the millennial generation. It shows a commitment to social responsibility. Millennials are starting businesses that have a 'double bottom line.' In other words, they are designing sustainable well-founded business models that are also meant to have a significant positive social impact.

For example, Dosed.com was started by Daniel Fine and his younger brother, Jake. When Daniel was eleven, he learned that his younger brother Jake, seven at the time, had been diagnosed with type 1 diabetes. Rather than sit back idly, Daniel and Jake decided together to start a foundation called Brotherly Love and go about finding a cure.

So far they've raised two million dollars through their foundation. They've also gotten into business by starting this wonderful app called Dosed. The app monitors the amount of insulin in the body at any given time, so instead of having to guess your insulin level, you actually know. It's a terrific business idea that meets a market need as well as providing a genuine benefit that has the potential to help millions of people around the world.

In Sum

While these are only several exciting examples, and obviously not every member of the millennial generation is going to be a successful entrepreneur, I will say this: Millennials are clearly well on their way to changing the way we work, how we live, and the way we view the world.

So, the next time you hear someone criticize this great generation - possibly calling them precious little snowflakes, simply smile and say:

"No. Millennials are doing some really great things, and we need to value, cherish, and respect their great work."

There is an optimistic, entrepreneurial spirit in this upcoming generation that will have a profound impact in shaping our future.

SECTION TWO

THE SPIRIT OF AMERICA

CHAPTER SIX

BLESSED TO BE AN AMERICAN

...the United States is the beacon of hope and simply the best place to live in the world.

In America, you can be anything you want to be:

You can achieve what you want to achieve.

We live in the freest country in the world.

We have a strong and growing economy.

Compared to Other Countries

One measure of how great it is to be an American is to compare ourselves and our life here in America to the experience of others in countries around the world. It can be easy to get complacent and take what we have here in America for granted. Easy sometimes to think that the grass may just be greener elsewhere.

So, let's take a look? How do we actually measure up? A cursory glance paints a clear and compelling picture. While in nearly every country around the world, there will always be elites who enjoy a preferred status, for the everyday citizen, there is no finer place to live than right here in the U.S.of A.

- WESTERN EUROPE: It's not even close. Americans enjoy much greater freedom, a deeper respect for the individual and a much more pervasive sense of 'Can Do' optimism than citizens of Western Europe. Not surprisingly, the economies of Western Europe are relatively stagnant There is a maturing population and emerging social problems, driven in large part by an unprecedented wave of immigrants who, so far, have failed to assimilate. All of which is exacerbated by the abject failure of European leaders, elites and the media to recognize and address the issue. In Western Europe, there is a wistful reliving of the past rather than an enthusiastic embracing of the future. In sum, Western Europe just doesn't have the same vibrancy and vitality we have here in the United States.
- RUSSIA: It is not an overstatement to say that this is a country run principally today by oligarchs, former members of the KGB and the Communist Party. These

are the same folks who ran the old Soviet Union into the ground, hamstrung their economy with central planning and raided the nation's wealth to line their own pockets, . Need I say more? Well, there is more. Beyond the sheer economic mismanagement is the human cost. The gray, dark, drab existence in a totalitarian state has a dehumanizing impact that pervades a people. Inevitably impacting generations into the future. While the Russian people may hopefully be blessed with the spirit to recover from this travesty, we are blessed to be living in America rather than in Russia.

- CHINA: While China is experiencing rapid economic growth, still, there is very little freedom. The individual is under the control of the central government. There is no right to free speech. In fact, most Chinese citizens cannot even freely access the internet or even engage with the various forms of social media that we as Americans access on a daily basis. While the average Chinese citizen is gaining great access to material wealth, he or she still lives in a totalitarian state, devoid of individual freedom.

- AFRICA: In the developing countries of Africa, for many, it is hard to even get by. So very many people on the African continent struggle to make a living and attain even the most basic of life's necessities. For instance, in Africa's newest country South Sudan, the average per capita income is less than five dollars per day. Moreover, for decades, civil unrest and government corruption have plagued people throughout the majority of the continent and have thus stalled meaningful progress and development.

- LATIN AMERICA: The clearest indication of life in Latin America is to check the flow of immigration. Everyday people from Latin America are risking their lives crossing our border illegally in pursuit of a better life. People are coming to the United States from Latin America for good reason. They yearn for the freedom, the economic opportunities and the respect for the individual that we have here in America.

It is the dream, the lifetime aspiration of so many people from all around the world to come to the United States. While there will always be ways we can improve, there is a nearly universal belief – and it is well founded – the United States is the beacon of hope and simply the best place to live in the world.

So - just for fun, I put together a list of the **Top Ten Reasons (actually eleven)** why America is so great and why we are so very blessed to be Americans. I am sure you could put together your own list and even improve on what I have suggested below. But, here goes:

Reason Number One – It probably goes without saying ... it's our **freedom**. We are truly blessed to be so very free here in the United States.

Reason Number Two – It's our economy. We have **economic wealth as well as the economic freedom to create.** We have growth and abundance. Our economic engine helps provide hope and resources to so very many. It's really a great thing.

Reason Number Three – We have **opportunity. We can choose** to be whatever we want to be. We can dream our dreams. We can set our sights on our individual goals and then soar as we achieve them.

Reason Number Four – We're **entrepreneurial**. We are creative. We have imagination. We have the spark to figure out solutions to problems, start businesses and build great things.

Reason Number Five – We are a **sharing** country. We care about our fellow Americans - our neighbors and about those in need. Of all the countries in the world we're among the leaders in terms of charitable giving and trying to help those among us who are less fortunate.

Reason Number Six – We are a **forgiving** people. We are nation that is known for giving second chances. We understand when people trip up and want to reward them for having the courage to pull themselves up, come back and give it another try. Second chance? Hey why not? We like to root for the underdog.

Reason Number Seven – We're **tolerant**. For instance, we actively support the right of individuals to practice their religion or their lifestyle freely and to express their views openly, even though we may sometimes disagree. Americans are, therefore, free to pursue their own unique lifestyle and personal choices with nearly limitless discretion and with the knowledge that their right to do so will protected by the government. In so many countries, such tolerance simply does not exist.

Reason Number Eight - We're **generous**. We give millions (and billions) in foreign aid every year to countries around the world. We give freely, perhaps too freely, of our economic wealth – but nonetheless, as such, we are clearly the most generous nation in the world. In addition, it is also a fact, that whenever there is a natural disaster anywhere in the world, it is America who shows up first, with an helping hand and ready to support.

Reason Number Nine – As Americans, we are blessed to have wonderful **traditions.** We celebrate Thanksgiving. We honor the Fourth of July. These are rich traditions that families can enjoy and that bind our communities together.

Reason Number Ten – It's just plain **fun** to be an American. We love sports. We enjoy the outdoors, hunting, fishing, and camping. We have a great sense of humor. Whether you're a fan of Jimmy Fallon or whether you remember Jay Leno or even Johnny Carson, Americans can be light hearted and enjoy a good laugh. We even poke fun at our politicians on a daily and nightly basis.

Reason Number Eleven – Here is one last thought. And it's so very important. We are blessed to be Americans because of the great men and women who serve in our military and who risk their lives to protect us. We are also blessed because of our police officers, firefighters and first responders who keep us safe in our communities. It is such a great feeling of pride when we have the opportunity to stand at attention and honor our flag as our national anthem is being played.

And on a personal note, the list would not be complete without mentioning the exhilaration so many of us feel when standing in a stadium and experiencing the sheer awe of a flyover – when our F-18's fly over the stadium reminding us of our freedom and the great dedication of our fine men and women in the armed services who keep us safe and free 24/7.

We are truly blessed to be Americans.

CHAPTER SEVEN

SMALL TOWN VALUES

Whether you grew up in a big city, small town or out in the suburbs, 'small town values' form the foundation of our American culture. These are the values that permeate a community, create shared values and build the bonds to endure for generations.

It was a time when kids could even feel free to walk to school.

I was raised in a small town. I grew up in Newport, New Hampshire, a wonderful town of 5,000 people in the western part of the state. Newport, the county seat, had a bustling main street, and a strong sense of community. It was a special place to grow up. In short, it was the kind of place where just about everybody in town knew your name and you knew everybody else. You felt comfortable not locking your doors. It was a time when kids could even feel safe to walk to school.

Small Town Community

The sense of community was apparent in so many ways. For instance, at the annual town meeting in March, nearly everyone in town would come to the town hall. Some would be dressed in their best suits. Others would come straight from work in their work clothes. It was a time for discussion to decide the important town issues. We had to decide things like whether to buy another fire truck, raise property taxes, or deal with zoning issues. Everyone had an opportunity to speak their mind and have their voices heard.

It was a heterogeneous community. There were immigrant populations in our town. The two largest groups were the Fins from Finland and a very strong Greek community. Both would celebrate their cultures and worship in their local churches, and contributed a richness to the fabric of our community.

Small Town Spirit

There was also a great sense of town spirit. For example, the Newport Winter Carnival, held each year, with various forms of winter contests and festivities, including skating on the Newport town common every year. There was a tremendous spirit around our athletics, particularly our high school football team, the Newport Tigers. Our football team was source of pride for the town, winning championship after championship in their high school division, year after year.

In addition, there was an unabashed patriotism. You know, most of the fathers of the kids I grew up with actually served in World War II. Without question, this created a deep bond from their shared experience. And, there were many quiet heroes. Interestingly, most never spoke of their war stories.

One such silent hero, as I later found out, was my old Little League coach. He was a large and gentle man, standing about six feet and four inches. He owned a small local restaurant in town and as far as I know, never spoke a word about his service to our country. In fact, after all these years, it was purely by chance, only recently, I discovered this man actually was a hero in World War II. He was one of those brave soldiers who landed at Omaha Beach on D Day. If you have seen the great Stephen Spielberg movie, *Saving Private Ryan,* you can imagine what this man went through.

Well, it turns out, he was not only on the beach,

We had shared values, a strong sense of loyalty and a deep patriotism but he was commanding 600 men. And even more, he successfully won the surrender of a notorious German colonel. And remarkably, all the years I knew him, he never spoke about it. Nor did the other quiet American heroes who walked the streets of our town.

All of which speaks volumes about the fabric of this community. We had shared values, a strong sense of loyalty and a deep patriotism. I share these thoughts because it seems there was so much *right* about growing up in a small town. My sense is that these values in small towns across our country provided a 'glue' to bind us; as well as a bedrock foundation of strength. Of course, things weren't perfect, but I marvel at the pride, the spirit and the sense of shared values in Newport as throughout so many small towns across our country.

Today Things are Different

Times, however, have changed. Many small towns have been hit hard in recent years. It has been a tough economy. Main Streets have emptied out. The opioid crisis has been ravaging. Devastating many of the families we knew growing up. Somehow through it all though, however, the positive spirit continues to live. Waiting to be rekindled and eager to glow even more brightly going forward.

...the truth is, we have the power to seize our future and regain our momentum.

As I look out on America, I see many small towns like Newport that have gone through some tough times. Jobs have gone overseas or been replaced by technology. The main street shops have been replaced by Walmarts, Dollar Stores and strip malls at the end of town. National chains, rather than independent stores owned and operated by your neighbor down the street. So, it's not like it used to be – and in so very many ways.

Having said all this, however, the truth is we have the power to seize the initiative, regain momentum and reclaim our future. We can revitalize our 'small towns' and build upon the strong foundation provided by our 'small town values.' It will take inspiration and courage. However, I am fully confident that it can be achieved. It can!

I'm optimistic because I know the positive spirit and positive energy remains. We can overcome these difficulties if we remain vigilant, strong, dedicated and focused. To be successful, it will take consistent energy, a positive spirit and a will to win. However, it is absolutely achievable. And, without question, it is absolutely worth the effort.

CHAPTER EIGHT

THE MAN IN THE ARENA

The 'Man in the Arena' is a phrase attributed to President Theodore Roosevelt. It relates to a passage from a speech he made in 1910, shortly after finishing his second term as President. While on a tour of Europe, and speaking to an audience in France, he said:

"It is not the critic who counts; not the man who points out how the strong man stumbles, or where the doer of deeds could have done them better. The credit belongs to the man who is actually in the arena, whose face is marred by dust and sweat and blood; who strives valiantly; who errs, who comes short again and again, because there is no effort without error and shortcoming; but who does actually strive to do the deeds; who knows great enthusiasms, the great devotions; who spends himself in a worthy cause; who at the best knows in the end the triumph of high achievement, and who at the worst, if he fails, at least fails while daring greatly, so that his place shall never be with those cold and timid souls who neither know victory nor defeat."

What does it mean? Well, it is one of my own personal favorites – and here's what it means to me...

In essence, it says that the real joy in life comes from the striving. The quest. Daring to do great things. To try. To struggle. Spending yourself in the quest to achieve your

We have the freedom, the will and the opportunity to go out there and try to make it happen.

mission, fulfill your purpose, and attain your goals. We each have our own individual missions and goals, and the joy comes from the pursuit. We have the freedom, the will and the opportunity to go out there and try to make it happen. Striving mightily.

And of course, in doing so, it's also important to bear in mind one stark reality. Sometimes you're going to fail. It's all part of the adventure.

So, you risk the failure. Risk the embarrassment. Risk what the critics might say. We all face the biting, harsh words of the critics because, inevitably, we all fail. But who wants to be one of them. The critics. Those poor and timid souls? Those are the people who are on the sidelines and do not dare to enter the arena at all.

On the face of it, the critics might most naturally be thought to be cowards. Lacking the basic courage to enter the arena. And I suppose there is some truth to this. However, I believe they are more accurately characterized as 'conformists.' Conforming to the general skepticism and doubts of the crowd while lacking the individuality and independent will to get into the arena and pursue their dreams. As timid souls, standing on the sidelines, they will never know the great triumphs available only to those who pursue great

If we step into the arena, we have this glorious opportunity - a wonderful chance to know the great triumphs and victories, or at the very least know we have expended ourselves in a worthy cause.

57

purpose while risking embarrassment and defeat.

Progress in America

Thank goodness for the 'man in the arena.' When you think about it, all progress is the result of efforts undertaken by those who have the courage to take the risks and step into the arena. It is driven by those who are willing to chase their dreams. No matter the cost; no matter the barbs, the slings, the arrows from the timid 'know it all' critics standing in safe unison on the sidelines.

Fortunately, in America, we celebrate those who step into the arena. In America, we are a nation of risk-takers. We like to participate and we like to get involved. In fact, our whole system of government is based on citizen participation. Getting involved in the democratic process.

And, this tradition goes way back to our earliest days. In the early 1800's, when the French historian Alexis de Tocqueville came to the United States, he marveled at the American people. At the extent to which we like to get involved. Throughout our history, we have been a nation of entrepreneurs, volunteers, active citizens, charitable givers, civic minded community leaders and the like.

Some will look around among us and bemoan the political system. They note divisiveness and apathy. But the truth is there has never been a better time - with more opportunity to get involved and actually step into the arena than there is today. And, in so doing, to make a difference and to help drive progress.

There are so many vitally important areas – where there is an opportunity to step into the arena and make a difference. Honoring and helping veterans. Assisting the homeless or those with substance abuse. Taking a leading role in education. Initiating programs to help underprivileged youth. There are so many opportunities, whether helping those in our inner cities or helping those in rural America. It can be said that "The morality of a society is defined by the treatment of the disadvantaged" ...Welcome to America! We all have this opportunity to get involved and make a difference.

Ultimately, it is up to each and every one of us. You can choose to step into the arena? Or choose to stake out a safe, but cold and lifeless, place for yourself among the critics. It's up to you. It's the most important decision you will ever make.

If we each choose wisely – and decide to step into the arena, we each have a glorious opportunity – the chance to know great triumphs and victories, or at the very least to know we have expended ourselves in a worthy cause.

CHAPTER NINE

SECOND CHANCES

In America we cheer second chances. We love the comeback. We love to root for the underdog. And it's a good thing because cheering for the underdog and giving second chances gives people the encouragement to persevere. People want to know that if they work hard, if they fight, and if they rise to life's challenges, they have the chance to succeed.

Abraham Lincoln's Second Chance

Abraham Lincoln is thought by many to be our greatest president, as well as one of the most important figures in all of American history. Not only did he preserve the Union, keeping America together, but he led the way in ridding the nation of slavery and extending basic freedoms to a whole new set of American citizens. However, if it were not for second chances, Abraham Lincoln would have never had the opportunity to achieve these great accomplishments.

Failure and Second Chance #1: In 1832, Lincoln ran for election to the Illinois State Legislature. He was defeated. And, could have easily called it quits. However, this defeat didn't stop him. In 1834, he was given a 'second chance' running for the same office, and this time, winning election. Lincoln then went on to win a series of successive re-elections serving four terms over the next eight years in the Illinois State Legislature.

Failure and Second Chance #2: After a brief hiatus, in 1843, Lincoln set his sights one step higher, and made a run for Congress – only to be defeated before even getting his party's nomination. Showing grit and determination, however, he decided to run again for the same seat in 1846. Winning the election, Lincoln served one two-year term in Congress representing his district from southern Illinois.

Failure and Second Chance #3: After taking a brief break from politics, in 1858, Lincoln attempted to take a significant step upwards, launching a campaign to run for the United States Senate. He ran a hard fought campaign but lost, being defeated by Stephen Douglas in a contest that was closely followed by the national media. While many men might have called it quits after suffering such a public defeat, Lincoln set his sights even higher, deciding to run for President of the United States. Remarkably, this recently defeated, one term congressman from Illinois believed so strongly in his vision and in himself that he persevered. Thankfully, Americans rallied to support him in his efforts, granting this repeat 'loser' yet another second chance and electing him to be the sixteenth President of the United States.

Lincoln's experience is so emblematic of the American spirit. A spirit that supports and enables second chances – allowing individuals to achieve their full potential. And it's not only true in politics, but also true in business.

Steve Jobs' Second Chance

Take, for instance, the case of Steve Jobs, the wonderfully celebrated creator and founder of Apple Computer. When Jobs, along with his partner Steve Wozniak, founded Apple in 1976, it was a revolutionary development, and by 1985, the company had achieved great success. Jobs was riding high and with his leadership at Apple, was clearly the darling of the personal computer revolution. Then, somewhat unpredictably in a boardroom coup, Jobs was suddenly ousted. The founder and CEO was unceremoniously dismissed from his own company. Ouch!

For many, this would've been the end of the line, but it's all about second chances and the human will to succeed.

After a brief hiatus, Jobs put his energies into founding another company called Next and dedicated himself to the venture. However, always with the gnawing memory of the unhappy ending and forced departure from Apple. Then, in 1997, Steve Jobs was presented with an opening. An opportunity to truly make his comeback. Apple's fortunes had deteriorated badly, and the company found itself on the brink of bankruptcy. Remarkably, Apple came back to Steve and said, *"We're going to give you a second chance. We want you to lead this company."*

He did, and in so doing, had the opportunity to leave his mark on the world. During his 'second chance,' Jobs led the way in creating such breakthrough innovations as the:

- iPod
- iTunes
- Apple Store
- iPhone

Hundreds of millions of individuals around the world benefitted from the 'second chance' that had been given to Steve Jobs.

Second Chances in Daily Life

Now, think about second chances in your daily life. It's not just these big-picture examples like Abraham Lincoln and Steve Jobs. In your own experience,

When you think about it, second chances are a really good thing. It gives everyone the hope and idea that if they try hard and work hard; they can come back and succeed.

you know businesspeople who have had terrible failures,

only to come back and succeed. You may also know people who have been convicted of crimes, served their time, paid their debt, and have come back to be productive members of our society.

Other people have had substance abuse problems or other failures in their personal life. They not only deserve a second chance, but we enthusiastically cheer their comeback. We want to give them a second chance. We support them and encourage their positive 'can do' spirit as they claw their way back.

The same is true of people in all walks of life. We, as Americans, cheer the grit and determination of the person who can overcome a setback, set his or her sights on a comeback – and ultimately succeed in doing so.

When you think about it, second chances are a really good thing. It gives everyone the hope and inspiration that if they try hard and work hard; they can come back and succeed.

So, let's continue to root for that underdog. Let's make sure we give everyone the second chance we all deserve. In doing so, we instill a sense of perseverance and pride which ultimately creates a positive, contagious energy that moves us forward as a people.

So, the next time you stumble or fail, as inevitably we all do, remember that in America, and increasingly in the rest of the world...we are given second chances. If you work hard, strive, and make a determined 'come back,' Americans will be cheering for you and your well-deserved success.

CHAPTER TEN

COMING TOGETHER

We have rarely been more divided as a nation than we are right now in America.

As I look out on the country we see Republicans versus Democrats. We see conservatives versus liberals or progressives. We see Right versus Left. We see division on so many other dimensions as well. This divisiveness and all of the negative energy surrounding our political discourse not only doesn't feel good, but in your heart you know that it can't be good for our country.

Thankfully, I don't believe it has to be this way. But right now, the fact is, there are bitter divisions within our country, and the first step forward in healing our divisions is to understand some of the root causes. While there is no single cause, there are a number of contributing factors. Here are just a few:

- Part of the divisiveness is structural. On both the right and the left, there is an infrastructure comprised of major donors, interest groups and thought leaders who line up on either side of the divide. They tend to support candidates and spokespersons at one extreme or the other – thus providing strong incentive for players to take extreme positions in support of their own personal advancement. This is particularly true of many interest groups who earn their continued existence – not by seeking common ground and solving problems – but by staking out extreme positions and seeking grievances to exploit as issues for political gain by stoking the emotions of their base.

- We also have the media divide. For instance, on one side of the spectrum we have MSNBC, the New York Times, CNN and others. On the other side is Fox News, The Wall St. Journal, Rush Limbaugh et al. More and more people are tuning in to the side of the media that is telling the story they already believe in. Their selection of media thus tends to reinforce their position, energize their passion and further harden the division. In turn, the media understanding this phenomenon and in the relentless pursuit of ratings, feeds into these emotions by selecting and accentuating news items that resonate with either side.

- Gerrymandering adds to the issue. The way we've set up districts in Congress doesn't help in the pursuit of common ground. Congress is principally comprised of safely Republican districts and safely Democrat districts – with very few congressional districts that are seriously contested. In other words, the overwhelming majority of Representatives to Congress tend to represent districts whose political leanings tilt strongly one way or the other, thus further polarizing the political system.

It's Becoming Increasingly Personal

And, it's not simply the issues. I don't know if you're seeing what I'm seeing, but the division is becoming much more personal. People on the right and on the left are seeing people on the other side, not simply as people who disagree with them. Instead, increasingly each is now viewing those on the other side of an issue as 'bad people' harboring evil intentions. And, when it gets personal like this, progress becomes so very difficult to achieve.

Rehashing Same Issues

Moreover, we have politicians who keep rehashing the same issues. Year after year, without any resolution. Focusing on issues where there is sharp divide and intense political debate. Thus, covered by the media as 'headline news.' But, no resolution in sight. Serving so much more like political theater being carried on in Washington, D.C. rather than serving the interests everyday Americans.

Indeed, wouldn't it be refreshing to change the focus of the debate – to transcend the endless discourse of the political class and to direct our attention to the issues that really matter? In truth, we actually do have an opportunity to change the political debate and transcend the bitter divide and the ugly discourse. To focus our energies on the positive – with a 'Can Do' attitude and address the issues that can impact our daily lives.

When it comes right down to it, I believe there is broad consensus as to what we as Americans really care about, need and want. Not only for ourselves, but for our families and future generations. Values and aspirations upon which we can build a bright and hopeful future.

To that end, I believe we are united in desiring the following.

We want an America where we can all be:

- Free
- Safe
- Healthy
- Fed
- Educated, and
- Productive

These are the core, fundamental issues. We want to feel free and safe. We want our families to be healthy and have food on the table. And, we want to educate our children so they can have an opportunity for even a better life than we've had.

With this in mind, let's agree to fundamentally alter the political discourse. Let's get away from the tired, bitter debate – and all the divisiveness that goes along with it. Let's transcend the issues that mesmerize and garner the attention of the political class. Instead, let's focus our energies like a laser. Let's apply all our efforts to addressing the basic issues that Americans really care about and can move our country forward. With a positive spirit and a 'Can Do' approach.

Individual Independence

And, in pursuing this path, let's make sure we do so to so in a way that unleashes the enormous power of the individual. Let's not revert to government as the first or only solution to all our problems. The greatest and most lasting way to solve so many of these issues is to harness the power of individual Americans, while also leveraging supportive families and local communities, non-profits, faith based organizations and entrepreneurs.

In sum, if we can transcend the current debate and raise our thinking to a higher level, we have the opportunity to solve real problems, improve real lives and change the course of history. And in so doing, we can heal the bitter divide, bring a positive energy to our political discourse and find greater unity as a people.

SECTION THREE

IF YOU BELIEVE – YOU CAN ACHIEVE

CHAPTER ELEVEN

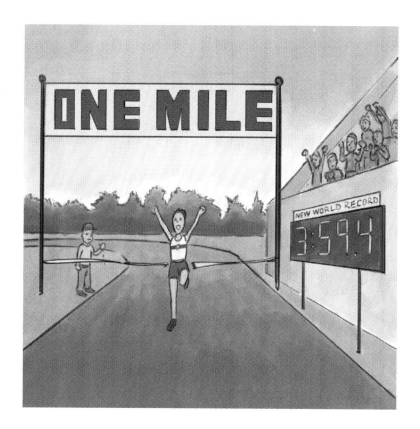

POWER OF BELIEF

It's often said that 'thoughts are things.' Powerful things, Maybe they are the only things... A thought can create a picture of possibilities. If we have a clear view of what the picture is, we can go out and achieve it. In other words, if we can *believe*.... we can *achieve*!

This is such a compelling vision of the world. And, I love one particular example of how it actually works. It's the amazing story of the four-minute mile.

Roger Banister and the Four Minute Mile

For decades, it was considered humanly impossible to run a mile in under four minutes. Many had tried and failed. In fact, doctors and physicians said a man might even die trying to run a mile in under four minutes.

Then came Roger Banister, a medical student at Oxford University who declared his mission to break the four-minute barrier. He developed a strong belief that he could achieve this goal. Keep in mind... most said it was impossible, and those few who thought it might be possible said the conditions – the weather, temperature, humidity, wind, the track, etc. – would have to be perfect in order even to have a chance at succeeding.

Because Banister was able to break the four-minute mile, others began to believe they could do the same thing. Incredibly, by the end of 1957, just three years later, an additional 15 people had broken the four-minute mile.

Bannister trained hard and finally made his attempt at the four minute mile in the spring of 1954. The young medical student started the day working at a hospital in London, then taking the train up to Oxford, with his race set for 6pm later in the afternoon. The day was anything but perfect. The wind was howling at 15 miles an hour when Roger Banister stepped onto the track at Oxford University on Iffley Road in the late afternoon looking to make history. It was a four-lap race, and after three laps, he was more than a full second off the required pace. However, something happened on that last lap.

With 275 yards to go, he began a late surge. Finishing the race in 3 minutes 59.4 seconds, thus shattering the heretofore seemingly impossible barrier. Bannister had broken the four-minute mile.

Beyond Belief

This power of Bannister's achievement, propelled by unwavering belief, is truly inspirational. It seems it was the power of his belief that allowed him to achieve.

Now, what's even more interesting is what happened next. Because Banister was able to break the four-minute mile, others then also began to believe they could do the same thing. Incredibly, by the end of 1957, just three years later, an additional 15 people had broken the four-minute mile. This is after *decades* of no one accomplishing this feat. Furthermore, just ten years later, the four-minute mile had become so seeped into the conscious mind as a 'doable' achievement, a high school athlete from Kansas named Jim Ryan was able to break the four-minute barrier in 1964.

On a personal note, I have first-hand knowledge that even the track in Oxford where Bannister ran his famous race was not a very good track. In 1978, I watched a race there. It was a one-mile race between college athletes, and in the crowd was Sir Roger Banister. The athlete who won that day actually ran the mile in under four minutes. In honor of Banister's earlier achievement, the crowd cheered and asked Sir Roger to do a victory lap with the winner of the race, and he did. So, I had the wonderful pleasure of seeing Roger Banister run around the same track. What a great thrill! And so interesting that by that time, it had become somewhat commonplace for accomplished runners at various levels to break the four-minute barrier.

John F. Kennedy - A Man with Vision

The story of Bannister's belief and what happened thereafter to open the floodgates for so many additional 'believers' and therefore 'achievers,' powerfully demonstrates how one's beliefs shapes what is possible for the individual to achieve.

On another dimension, it is also possible for one person to vividly paint a vision with such strong conviction and clarity that it is imbued and adopted by others, who in turn become the believers and achievers that cause the vision to be realized.

One such example occurred in the 1960's. A newly elected President John F. Kennedy set a vision, a goal for America in 1961. In a speech to a joint session of Congress, Kennedy shared his vision. He set a goal for the United States to land a man on the moon, and bring him safely back to earth, by the end of the decade.

I think many may have been skeptical at first but began to believe as the decade went on.

Kennedy's vision had set in motion a series of activities that gathered momentum and helped to crystallize this belief into reality. As a result, in 1969, Neil Armstrong and Buzz Aldrin landed on the moon and, in fact, did return safely back to earth. Believed and achieved.

The Power of Belief in Nations

It is also this power of belief that allows nations to achieve great victories in times of crisis. Recently, I was talking to a friend who had just lost his mother. She had lived to a very advanced age, and as we were talking, he recalled some of the most memorable conversations he had with her.

My friend is a student of history, and knowing his mother had lived through the time of World War II, here in the United States, he asked her:

" Mom, what was it like with Hitler's armies beginning to sweep through Europe in the early 1940's, looking as though they might even conquer Europe, win the war and achieve world domination? Were you scared? Did you ever think America might lose?"

Without hesitation, she responded:

" No. We all always knew we were going to win."

Wow! Imagine that. Such a strong and universal belief. In retrospect, on a purely objective basis, there may have been room to doubt what the outcome would be. However, the American people had a fervent, unwavering belief. We were going to win. And, so it came to be.

In Sum

The power of belief is an amazing force. And, thoughts are the things that originate and create this force. As such, we each have the opportunity to create beliefs for ourselves and thus achieve great things. It starts with a thought.

The thought then over time forms a belief. And, if the belief is held firmly enough and with strong enough conviction, it puts in motion a series of actions, allowing the belief to come into reality.

...let's remove the limits and do all we can to fulfill the full potential of the human capability. Thoughts are powerful things.

Each of us has the opportunity to tap into this power of belief. We can access it for ourselves in much the same way as did Roger Bannister. We can set in motion great visions through this power as exemplified by President Kennedy in getting us started and on the way to the moon.

And, this is particularly exciting when we think about the positive good, the positive energy, we can harness when we form aspirational and inspiring beliefs. As is often said, we are limited only by our beliefs. With this in mind, let's remove the limits and do all we can do fulfill the full potential of the human capability. Thoughts are powerful things.

CHAPTER TWELVE

THE POWER OF POTENTIAL

Have you ever wondered what's your true human potential? If you were really hitting on all cylinders what could you accomplish? What if you were operating at your full mental potential, physical potential, and spiritual potential? Imagine how strong you could be.

Examples of Physical Potential

Now, we've all heard stories of incredible feats of strength under life-or-death circumstances. Here are a couple of my favorites – truly amazing.

Angela Cavallo, an ordinary housewife, was in her home folding laundry as her son, Tony, worked outside on his '64 Chevy Impala. Suddenly, as the jack moved, she heard the car come crashing down on him. This is the incredible part - she rushed out, picked up the 1,100-pound car and held it four inches off the ground for *five minutes*. Imagine that? It makes you wonder. What's the true potential of your physical power?1

Another example I like, partly because of the name of the man who did the rescuing, happened on the set of the television show *Magnum P.I.*

There was an episode involving a helicopter, and most people who watched the show would not know this, but one of the passengers got trapped in the helicopter underwater as it was performing a stunt. He was pinned and was clearly not going to survive unless somehow the helicopter could be moved and he could be released.

Unbelievably and almost out of nowhere the passenger's coworker, whose name is Tiny (You'll understand the appropriateness of the name if you watch the YouTube video), picked the helicopter up out of the water. This helicopter weighed nearly 2000 pounds. He literally picked up the 2,000 pound helicopter! It was absolutely amazing. And, please do watch the video.

Examples of Mental Potential

There are also a number of almost unbelievable examples where mental strength rather than physical capacity is put to the test. You've probably heard the following statement: 'At any given time, we're only operating with a small percentage of our mental capability.' Some say it's only 5 percent, while others say 10 percent, but *no one* says we are operating at full strength. It makes you wonder about the true potential?

Here's one interesting example that begins to provide a clue. You may remember the movie *Rain Man,* which starred Dustin Hoffman. Interestingly, he actually was playing a real person named <u>Kim Peek, a real-life super genius</u>. It's an illustration of the potential of the human mind.

Imagine this. Kim read approximately 12,000 books during his lifetime, but more than that, he actually retained 98 percent of the information from his reading. You might ask "how is it that someone is able to even read 12,000 books? To put this in perspective, if you could read a book every single day, 12,000 books would take almost thirty-three years of consecutive reading.

So how did he do it? Here's the secret. Kim was able to read two pages *every eight seconds*. He would use his left eye to read the left page and right eye to read the right page, and have them memorized within eight seconds.

The American Potential?

In the cases I've described, you may come away thinking that these people were born with super human *Ask the question, what if we as a people had the ability to tap into our full potential? What could we create? What could we achieve?* strength or mental capacity. Therefore, markedly different from you and me. However, perhaps the opposite is true? Maybe we're more the same than different. Maybe we all have the same capacity or potential – but we just don't have the knowledge or ability to tap into our amazing strengths? Makes you wonder.

Now think about the United States of America. And, ask the question, what if we as a people had the ability to tap into our full potential? What could we create? What could we achieve?

Workforce Potential?

As a starting point, I believe that we are nowhere near performing to our full potential today. Recently, I had the pleasure to read a thought provoking book written by Jim Clifton, Chairman, and CEO of the Gallup organization, the great public research firm. In the book, titled <u>The Coming Job Wars</u>, Clifton asks a question about potential: 'What could we accomplish as a workforce if we were really engaged in our jobs?'

To figure this out, Gallup surveyed a sample of Americans, asking the following question: "Are you actively engaged in your employment or are you sort of disengaged?"

Remarkably, of the 100 million people in the United States who are actively working, only 28 percent feel engaged at work and truly feel they are productive. The other 72 percent are actively or somewhat disengaged – not firing on anything like 'all cylinders.'

It truly raises the question: Can you imagine the impact on the productivity of our country if we could take even one half of this 72 percent of our workforce that is disengaged and get them fully engaged? Thus, getting us closer to our potential as a nation? To put this in human terms, this would mean an increase of 36 million Americans becoming actively and fully engaged in their daily jobs.

Obviously, there would be far greater output. But think about the impact on the quality of the work produced. Those not engaged in their jobs are simply going through the motions. As soon as they clock in, their mind immediately turns to lunch, the end of the workday or some other non-work topic. As a result, there are more defects in their work and the level of customer service is nowhere near where it potentially could be.

Moreover, think about the impact on quality of life and personal satisfaction? Overall happiness? We have an important task in front of us.

Student Potential?

Another interesting, and frightening, statistic concerns our students. Of the 75 million students in our school system, there are nearly 20 million who fail to graduate from high school. Think about each of these 20 million young people going into the job market without a high school education. Consider how this impacts their job prospects going forward. Moreover, what is the impact on their future families and the lives their children will be able to lead? How will they think about the world?

Alternatively, just imagine, what if we could improve that number by half? And get 10 million of those students excited about school, provide the support they need and get them to graduate? What a great impact this would have on the lives of each of these individuals and their futures. What a profoundly positive achievement for our nation as a whole.

Healthcare Potential?

There is one more area I would like to mention - our healthcare system. In a recent survey of doctors, it was determined that nearly one half of all recommended procedures, hospitalizations, and tests may be unnecessary. In other words, these are being prescribed purely for defensive reasons. To put it bluntly, the doctors don't want to get sued. So, they order the unnecessary procedures and tests. What a terrible waste of time and money – not to mention the squandering of our scarce healthcare resources.

Meanwhile, the 'fix' is relatively straightforward. If we could reform our system of civil lawsuits, torts, and legal damages, we could reduce an enormous amount of waste. And, of course, tap into the true potential of our healthcare system. Imagine the impact. It's estimated we could save half a *trillion* dollars if we would simply eliminate these unnecessary procedures.

In Sum

In stepping back and thinking about the enormity of our human potential, whether it be physical or mental, it's worth asking the question: What if each of us could be performing at much closer to our true potential?

And, then, think of our American potential – what outcomes could we achieve as a people, as a

I think of our American potential – what outcomes could we achieve as a people, as a nation, if could truly tap into our full potential?

nation, if could truly tap into our full potential? I am struck by what enormous opportunities lie in front of us and the immensely positive rays of sunshine for our future if we can harness the energy to pursue them with vigor and enthusiasm.

CHAPTER THIRTEEN

POWER OF THE HUMAN SPIRIT

Each and every one of us has the ability to unleash the power of the human spirit. Every one of us has an individual goal, mission, or purpose in our lives. Living is all about unleashing our own human power to achieve that goal, mission, or purpose. It's all about how we advance, grow, and fulfill our full potential. I'd like to alert you to a danger, though. I see it in today's society here in America - a danger to us all as individuals.

American Sunshine

Reliance on the State Instead of the Individual

To do that, I'd like to cite a particular, powerful message I remember from a commercial aired during the Super Bowl in 1984 by Apple Computer. They were introducing the new Macintosh computer. The computer was going to be a powerful new way to inspire creativity on the part of the individual.

Here's the scene. Imagine an auditorium, almost like a movie theater, with a powerful face on the screen. It's the face of a dictator talking to the audience and describing what he portrays as a glorious future. A world where all people are as 'one' – all thinking alike, all acting alike, all in unison. As the camera pans out to the audience, you see an auditorium filled with gray lifeless people sitting in silent obedience. Immediately, you know that despite the promises of the dictator on the screen, this totalitarian world of 'one-ness' is not a happy place.

Suddenly, at that very moment, a woman athlete approaches the back of the theater. She comes running down towards the screen wielding a hammer, and she hurls it towards the screen. It hits the screen, creating a massive explosion.

It is a courageous act. An act of disobedience and incredibly liberating. Every time I think about the commercial, or see it again, I get excited. I get goosebumps because I see it as vividly demonstrating the power of the individual. The spirited lone soul who stands up to challenge a dominating authority demanding conformity.

I love this commercial because it sets up this really interesting contrast. On the one hand, the all-powerful state. On the other hand, the creativity of the individual. The powerful state may give you food, it may give you shelter and material things, but it demands lifeless conformity and snuffs out any kind of individuality. It takes away our freedoms and puts us in a miserable, gray existence.

Then there is the spirit of the individual. To have the freedom to make our own decisions and to fulfill our purpose in life. This is where true happiness comes from. True happiness cannot be attained simply by receiving the material goods a faceless state can give to you. Instead, true happiness comes from the opportunity for each and every one of us to work hard, strive, advance, grow, achieve and realize our dreams.

Earned Success

The greatest happiness in life comes from what I would call 'earned success.' This is the ability to go out, work on your goals, and make meaningful progress. In a state that dominates and doesn't allow you to make your own decisions, such happiness is virtually impossible to achieve. However, as an individual living in a free society, you can choose your path and make your own decisions. Thus making progress every day and taking meaningful steps towards fulfilling your dream and achieving your main mission in life.

For us as Americans, we need to be vigilant. We need to be vigilant in preserving the freedoms we were all born to enjoy. We need to be thoughtful in protecting our rights as individuals and stopping the encroachment of an ever-growing state that is in part propelled by the purpose to grow and maintain its own existence.

Indeed, let's celebrate our freedoms. Let's celebrate the positive energy and individuality we can each enjoy. And, like the courageous woman in the Apple commercial, let's boldly defend ourselves from any encroachment on our freedoms. Always resisting mindless conformity as we unleash the power of the human spirit.

CHAPTER FOURTEEN

INSPIRATION AND ASPIRATION

These two words, inspiration and aspiration, sound very similar. Both are vitally important to achieving success.

However, they have very different meanings:

- **Inspiration** is all about the mental stimulation. It's about the energy you feel when you want to go achieve something. You get stimulated internally and say, "Hey, I'm inspired."

- ***Aspiration***, on the other hand, is about your goal. It's says, "I aspire to achieve something in particular."

Yet, they work together. It is difficult, perhaps impossible, to achieve success without practicing these two elements 'hand in hand.'

Explanation

Have you ever seen somebody who really has no particular goal in mind? Have you noticed their body language, perhaps seen them lying on the couch? They appear to be kind of lifeless actually. Then, all of the sudden they set a goal or perhaps we help set one for them. At that point, they have aspiration. They have something they want to achieve. Their entire body language changes. There's a new spring in their step. Life becomes a bit of a fun adventure. There's something to live for...something to strive for...something to go achieve.

It also works the other way around. Imagine another person who is also just lying on the couch. For whatever reason they develop a feeling internally of inspiration. They are inspired! They begin looking at the world very differently. Instead of not being able to see any opportunity at all, they see opportunities all over the place. They choose one – or several – of these opportunities to set as their goal. The inspiration links up with a specific aspiration.

Section Three - If You Believe – You Can Achieve

Examples

As mentioned in a previous chapter, back in the early 1960's President Kennedy set a goal of sending a rocket ship into space, landing a man on the moon and returning him safely back to earth by the end of the decade. It was an aspiration – a goal. In so doing, he inspired a whole generation of young people – scientists, engineers and others to go accomplish this mission. And, of course, in 1969, the mission was successfully accomplished. This is a wonderful example of a clearly defined and well-articulated aspiration then inspiring a nation to accomplish an historic feat. I find this to be an especially powerful example of aspirational goal setting due to the way it was articulated when the vision was first shared.

Speaking at Rice University, in September 1962, Kennedy stated:

"We choose to go to the moon. We choose to go to the moon in this decade and do the other things, not because they are easy, but because they are hard, because that goal will serve to organize and measure the best of our energies and skills, because that challenge is one that we are willing to accept, one we are unwilling to postpone, and one which we intend to win, and the others, too."

What a powerful vision. And to choose this aspirational goals "not because they are easy, but because they are hard..." You can palpably feel the energy that must have been set in motion by this exhilarating aspiration.

Meanwhile, for Dr. Martin Luther King, his gift was inspiration. Dr. King inspired a generation of African Americans to go achieve. He inspired them with a dream. With the inspiration to take the first steps along a glorious path forward, with almost limitless potential. In doing so, Dr. King's inspiration unleashed a generation to seek their own individual goals and chart a course to achieve them.

...these are examples of how inspiration and aspiration work together on a very large scale. But, the two are also vitally important to achieving success in your daily life.

Colin Powell rose to become our first African American Secretary of State. And, shortly thereafter, Condoleezza Rice became the first African American woman to hold that same office.

In addition, Dr. Ben Carson who became one of the world's leading neurosurgeons with breakthrough procedures in pediatric surgery. And, of course, the most shining example, in 1968 the election of our first black President, President Barack Obama. A generation of achievement set in motion, in part due to the inspirational impact of Dr. King.

In Sum

So, take a moment and think back. Reflect on your own personal achievements. Consider how these two forces –

inspiration and aspiration - have worked together 'hand in hand' to propel you forward. Also, think for just a bit about how you might share your insights with others to give them the inspiration to get 'fired up' to go achieve? How you might help them develop an aspiration or a goal that will put them on the pathway to success. You have the opportunity to dramatically motivate and impact others by simply sharing your positive energy and putting them on course to achieve their true potential.

CHAPTER FIFTEEN

ABUNDANCE MENTALITY

An abundance mentality gives the perspective of seeing the glass half full instead of half empty. It's really the opposite of a scarcity mentality and it's much more than simply a way to look at the world outside ourselves. It's deep within our individual subconscious. With an abundance mentality you can actually believe great things are possible.

To make the concept come alive I want to talk about two different times in our nation.

A Time of Scarcity

In the 1970's, the United States developed a scarcity mentality. President Carter was in office and it seemed everything was going bad:

- We had an energy shortage
- Inflation was out of control
- Interest rates were near 20 percent
- There was a national spirit of malaise

Once you begin to go in this direction, it becomes a self-fulfilling prophecy. Things get worse and worse and worse. As an individual, you can feel it in your body posture. You tense up, get all tight and things appear very negative. For someone with a scarcity mentality, the solution to our national economic problems of the time would be to preserve, to use less, to avoid running out. Interestingly, very much in line with what President Carter actually did, as he signaled scarcity to the nation in announcing that he would turn down the thermostat at the White House. Obviously, driven by a scarcity mentality.

A Time of Abundance

By contrast, in the 1980's, led by the infectious optimism of Ronald Reagan, Americans developed an abundance mentality. Famously, it was the 'Morning in America.' We embraced the idea that if we can have the confidence to believe, we can achieve. We can actually succeed.

The 1980's unleashed an incredible economic boom for the United States. But it really wasn't just about economics. It was about confidence.

- And with confidence your posture changes.
- You open up to possibilities.
- You get more energy.
- You get a smile.
- Things are going to be good.
- You believe things will be good and they become good

Again, this is self-fulfilling prophecy in the other direction and it takes on great momentum.

Personal Abundance Mentality

This positive momentum you enjoy when you're experiencing the abundance mentality takes many forms. One form is what I call entrepreneurial creativity. It's when you really believe you can achieve things. You can be an entrepreneur. You maybe don't know what the answer is when you start. But – if you have this subconscious belief you can be successful, you can actually invent new ways of doing things. You find solutions to problems. Although they may be difficult problems, you have the strength to overcome them.

Starving Masses Predicted

In the late 1700's, an economist by the name of Thomas Malthus predicted the world would run out of food. He observed the world's growing population would create such demands on our food supply it would result in starvation, famine and death...terrible things. Well, of course we all know it didn't happen. The reason it didn't happen is in part due to a belief in abundance. A mentality that consistently allows us to find new and interesting solutions to problems and work our way out of difficult situations.

The Issue of Tax Cuts

Now, let me take this same mentality of abundance and apply it to today's fiscal problems in the United States.

Back in the 1960's, President Kennedy proposed a series of tax cuts. By reducing taxes he allowed more money to stay in the economy to be invested. It grew the economy, produced more jobs and grew the overall capability of our government to afford things.

There will always be people who have a scarcity mentality who will tell you if you cut taxes, you must also cut spending. Where are you going to find the money?

Well, that's not the way it works. In the real world, things work in a much more dynamic way. What really happens when you cut people's taxes is that they have more money. They use the money to spend and to invest. In turn, the money creates jobs. It's like a roaring engine propelling the economy forward. And, of course, the growing economy ends up generating more tax revenues – not less.

It's why President Kenney proposed tax cuts in the 1960's.

It's why President Reagan did the same in the 1980's.

And, it is the driving force that has consistently put us on the path to the greatest economic expansions in the history of the United States. It is why tax cuts work. It starts with an abundance mentality. The initial progress and access to capital inspires confidence. Tension melts away. And a self-reinforcing momentum propels us forward.

As I step back and think about the two views of the world - scarcity versus abundance, I see a striking similarity to another concept. The notion that 'if you believe, you can achieve.' If you have a strongly positive attitude and it seeps deep into your subconscious, without even knowing it, you're going to be able to achieve things you never dreamed possible. It's really the magic of the abundance mentality. And, happily, it can work for us as a nation as well as for each of us as individuals.

CHAPTER SIXTEEN

VICTIM MENTALITY

I'm sure there have been times in your life when you have felt like a victim. You've been wronged or hurt and it wasn't your fault.

It's so very easy to get discouraged, blame a specific person – or just blame the world in general. We can wallow in self-pity. We can seek out solace and support from a friend or mentor who even plays into these feelings, legitimizes our 'victimhood.' This way of thinking may even explain why we may see ourselves as a member of some oppressed class. Feels good, right? For a while....

But, deep down, you know it's not right, you're not really justified. In fact, choosing to be a victim runs directly in contrast to the 'power of belief' that lets us overcome obstacles. It also runs directly against the grain of the American 'Can Do' spirit and the bedrock optimism that has made our country great.

For instance, during the 1700's, around the time of the American Revolution, a young man came into prominence. His name was Paul Revere. H was a well-known Boston silversmith and immortalized in a poem penned by Henry William Wordsworth celebrating his patriotic nighttime ride warning fellow colonists of the advancing British army. Having achieved such a station in life, you would have thought he had enjoyed an advantaged upbringing. However, it was not the case. He was born to a family of twelve children. His older brother didn't survive into adulthood. Young Paul even had to leave school at the age of thirteen, becoming an apprentice to a silversmith. It was hardly an easy beginning.

However, he approached life with energy and optimism. He excelled in his trade. He rose to become a leader in the emerging opposition to British rule. Winning great respect as a member of the Massachusetts Committee on Safety – a vital and motivating force in the American Revolution. Paul Revere chose not to be a victim.

The American Tradition:

Overcoming Difficult Beginnings – Refusing to be a Victim

In the 1800's in America, Horatio Alger wrote 'rags-to-riches' stories for young adults. His stories depicted people who had risen from very humble beginnings to do extraordinary things. Alger's stories resonated with the public largely because they embodied a 'Can Do' spirit that was deeply rooted in the American way of life. These stories were also validated by the numerous real life 'rags to riches' examples of success that personified the era. For instance, during the late 19th century, Andrew Carnegie arrived from Scotland, with little more than a positive attitude and a strong work ethic and went on to become one of the wealthiest men in all of America.

John D. Rockefeller, Henry Ford and inventors like Alexander Graham Bell and Thomas Edison also rose to prominence from very humble beginnings and each had to overcome obstacles that could easily have defeated them.

In fact, Thomas Edison especially could have claimed to be a victim. He had very poor hearing. He had limited formal education. But he went on to become one of the greatest inventors of all time.

Victimless Leaders of Today

Even today, we tend to celebrate people like Steve Jobs and Bill Gates, the creators of Apple and Microsoft. It's easy to forget that neither of them graduated from college. They both worked long hours, working in cubicles with no early indication of their ultimate success. But they kept right at it.

In fact, as earlier described, Steve Jobs was even fired from his own company. From Apple... Now, there's a guy who could've been a victim! Instead, he set his sights on coming back. And he did so with gusto – helping Apple to create millions of happy users and impacting people around the world.

We celebrate the American spirit with so many vivid examples. Inspirational, powerful illustrations of the human spirit – refusing to be a victim.

- Rosa Parks got on a bus in Montgomery, Alabama in 1955, in the segregated South at a time when "colored people" were meant to sit in the back of the bus. Rosa Parks said, "No, I'm going to sit where I want to sit and where I deserve to sit." Her courage, and outright refusal to be a victim, ignited one of the greatest transformations in American history, ultimately leading to the civil rights movement of the 1960's.

- Wilma Rudolph was a young girl born in 1940, growing up in rural Tennessee. At the age of four, she contracted polio. She lost the use of her left leg and her left foot. For the next six years, from the ages of four to ten, she had a brace on her left leg and was largely unable to move it.

  However, she had a goal. She wanted to excel in track. Through incredible strength and determination, she pushed herself - training hard to be a competitive sprinter. By the time she was 20-years-old she was an

Olympic athlete. She even won three gold medals at the Rome games in 1960. That's almost unbelievable! That's determination! That's saying 'I am not going to be a victim!'

- Dr. Ben Carson is a more recent example. He grew up in the inner city of Detroit. He had a dream. He wanted to become a doctor. Although he grew up in a fatherless family living on welfare and food stamps – he was determined. He earned a scholarship to Yale University and had a desire to practice medicine. He not only became a doctor, but rose to become one of the most famous and successful neurosurgeons in all the world, later even becoming a candidate for President of the United States.

What all these people have in common is that each one of them could have been a victim. Could've said, "Hey, life's not fair. I'm not going to go any further." Or even could've said, "I'm going to give up before I start."

But they didn't. They believed in the power of the human spirit.

Listen for Victim Words

- *I can't do something*
- *There are obstacles*
- *I don't have an opportunity*
- *I am being discriminated against*
- *Life is just not fair*

Maybe you've heard similar words coming out of your own mouth. And, to some extent these thoughts may bear an element of truth. However, it's also true that positive energy can overcome all of these negative victim thoughts and help achieve incredible outcomes.

They believed in the value of strength, determination and the immense power of their own potential. And, it's that same spirit that is available to all of us – if we just engage our positive energy – and embrace a 'Can Do' mentality.

As I look around America, I'm tremendously excited. I know there are vast reservoirs of positive energy. We all have the power to overcome difficult situations and achieve whatever we want to achieve if we can simply remove the shackles of the victim mentality.

The key is to embrace a deep and unwavering faith in the positive. To believe in the human potential. To have a sense of gratitude. And to unleash the power of the human spirit toward individuality, dignity, the quest for growth and ultimate freedom. And, in so doing, vanquish any vestiges of the victim mentality,

CHAPTER SEVENTEEN

PRACTICAL THOUGHTS
ABOUT BACK PAIN

Chances are, you have suffered from back pain some time during your life.

And, what a terrible way to live your life.

As you may be aware, I am a pretty determined runner. I absolutely love the physical exercise – but even more so the solitude, and the quiet time to think. However, a number of years ago, I started to develop pain in my lower back. As I continued with my daily runs, it got worse. Lots worse – including sciatica, with pain radiating and shooting down my right leg.

Of course, being a 'determined' runner, I was too stubborn to take a break. So, I kept on with my daily runs while it progressively got worse. It finally reached the point where I could barely walk or get out of bed in the morning. At that point, I had to call a halt.

In search of relief, I began a frantic search – exploring all sorts of treatments. Trying anything and everything. Physical therapy, yoga, stretching, core strength training, chiropractors, acupuncture, deep tissue massage, cortisone shots, pain medications, and even considering surgery. Nothing worked.

I had almost given up when I accidentally stumbled on to a most amazing treatment. Thank god, after a long search and a continuous series of dead ends, I finally found a cure to my back pain.

By the end of this chapter, I will share this incredible cure. However, I'd like to ease you into it slowly.

> *"Hearty laughter is a good way to jog internally without having to go outdoors."*
>
> *Norman Cousins*

So – let's start with a fundamental premise. You know, much of our physical health starts in the mind. It has been proven that many of our illnesses and sicknesses are really a result of the way we think. While, yes, there truly are debilitating illnesses, in many cases, perhaps most, they derive from the way the think. Enabled, caused, perhaps magnified by our thoughts.

Go back and study the Hindu and Buddhist religions. One of the life-extending practices of both cultures has been meditation. Meditation is a way to ease stress and stress is the root cause of much of our illness.

Biological Implications of Stress:

- It's been proven that stress inhibits our immune system.
- Stress impacts our DNA – in studies subjects have been put under stressful conditions with testing before and after the experience. As a result, we can see actual structural differences in the DNA.

Norman Cousins' Discovery

You may be familiar with the remarkable experience of Norman Cousins. In 1964, after a very stressful trip to Russia, he found himself in nearly constant pain. His doctor diagnosed him with a degenerative disease, confined him to a hospital bed and gave him only six months to live. The horrific illness had caused him already to lose the use of his arms, and his legs were deteriorating rapidly.

His response to the doctor's diagnosis was certainly unusual – but at the same time, creative and brilliant. Cousins reasoned that if stress and negative emotions had somehow contributed to his illness, then positive emotions should help him feel better. With his doctor's consent, he checked out of the hospital. From a hotel across the street, he began to take extremely high doses of Vitamin C while at the same time watching hour after hour of humorous films, comedies, jokes and whatever other funny things to make him laugh.

He said that after about 10 minutes of good belly laughing he would finally be able to enjoy approximately two hours of pain-free sleep. He had tried morphine and it had not given him this same level of relief. If laughter and positive thoughts were able to give Cousins more relief from pain that morphine, just imagine how much control we have over our physical bodies due to the way we think.

Cause of Back Pain

Now let's apply the same reasoning to back pain. It's been estimated that much of the cause of back pain is mental. In fact, some studies show up to 75 percent of the cases of back pain don't have any structural cause at all. In other words, there is no visible cause that can be identified by x-ray, MRI or other diagnostic procedures. Thankfully, Dr. John Sarno, a medical doctor, researcher and longtime practitioner in the area of back pain, has a theory. In his book, "Healing Back Pain – the Mind-Body Connection" , Dr. Sarno describes numerous case studies of patients who have been able to fully eliminate their back pain by simply recognizing the emotional roots of their pain and thus severe the connection between their mental and physical experiences.

Through his practice, Sarno's theory has consistently been proven right. Now, how does it all work? The simple answer: Our stress actually constricts the flow of blood to certain parts of our body – therefore triggering pain. Here's how it happens:

- You're in a stressful condition
- Maybe you're a type A personality (In fact, many of the people with back pain actually are type A people.)
- During the process of stress, the blood flow is constricted to certain parts of the body – your back for instance
- When the blood is constricted and the flow of blood is affected, there is pain in that part of the body and it won't go away
- Of course, the pain causes more stress
- Which causes more constriction
- Which causes more stress
- Which causes more constriction...
- Your body is in a sort of a "doom loop" of cause and effect...a vortex...

Dr. Sarno is essentially saying it's all in your head. What's his solution to the problem? Well, it may surprise you. He simply walks you through the reasoning and lets you know that the cause of the problem is coming from your own thoughts.

Magically, over a relatively short period of time, the back pain goes away.

I highly recommend you go to this YouTube video to see a segment from ABC's 20/20 program. Barbara Walters and John Stossel do a wonderful profile on Dr. John Sarno and some of his actual patients. Out of all the patients who have come to Dr. Sarno's office over the years, 75 percent have been cured...absolutely cured of their back pain. If you've ever had back pain, please do give it a try.

And, of course, as you probably have surmised by now, what was the answer to back pain for me? Yes, you guessed it, this is the cure that worked for me. A good friend tipped me off and suggested I find out about Dr. Sarno and his methodology. And, thankfully, only a short time later I was able to virtually eliminate the debilitating pain. Thank you, Dr. Sarno!

SECTION FOUR

TACKLING TOUGH CHALLENGES WITH POSITIVE ENERGY

CHAPTER EIGHTEEN

FREEDOM OF SPEECH

In America, freedom is our most precious value. At the very top of the list are our First Amendment freedoms. Freedom of speech. Freedom of expression. Freedom of religion. Freedom to share our views. It's the rock solid foundation of our democracy. It's absolutely essential to our workings as a free society. In fact, it's so vitally important, I would fight to the death to defend our right to freedom of speech.

Negative Trends

Surprisingly, there are some people amongst us who don't believe in free speech. Moreover, recently they have been taking actions to shut it down. For instance, at Middlebury College in Vermont, Dr. Charles Murray, a well-known author was physically prevented from speaking by a group of anti-speech protesters. In fact, it got so violent that some of the members of his party were seriously injured as a result.

On the west coast, at the University of California at Berkeley, Ann Coulter, a conservative author and commentator was invited to speak. When anti-speech protesters threatened to 'shut her down,' the university declined to protect her and ultimately disinvited her to the school campus.

These are disturbing events. Moreover, they are not isolated instances, but instead part of a broader trend threatening to undermine and greatly constrain our freedom of speech.

Constitutional Right

To view this trend in the proper context, it is worth remembering that freedom of speech is enshrined in a very special place within our Constitution. It is enumerated as the very First Amendment to our Bill of Rights precisely because it was viewed by our Founders as our most important right. In part it says, "Congress shall make no law abridging the freedom of speech or freedom of expression."

It's so vitally important. Imagine where we would be without it.

"Congress shall make no law abridging the freedom of speech or freedom of expression."

Imagine our political system without the protections which allow dissenting voices to be heard. In such a world, one party could easily become dominant and then use the instruments of government to squelch opposing views, prevent political discourse and effectively shut down all opposition. Thus, fully undermining the very basis for our democratic system of government.

In such a circumstance, those in power would not only have full control of our government apparatus but also the power to dominate our society. Without our freedom of speech, we as individual dissenters could suffer the same fate as that brave young man in Tiananmen Square in 1989 who faced down the Chinese army tanks and reportedly was later executed.

What Are You Afraid Of?

It should be so very clear that our right to free expression is fundamental. It is vitally important in itself – but also critical in helping to protect the functioning of our republic as well as all of the other freedoms we enjoy.

With this in mind, I would like to ask a simple question. I direct this question to any of those in our society who would consider trying to suppress our freedom of speech.

My question is: Why do you try to shut down and constrain free speech? What are you afraid of? What is the lasting harm of letting others express their opinions? If you have confidence in the validity and strength of your ideas, there's really nothing to be afraid of. Let the ideas be tested in the marketplace.

But therein lies the problem, doesn't it? It's clear: Those who actively try to shut down the expression of others actually lack confidence in the validity and strength of their own ideas. They are not confident their ideas will ultimately win – when fully scrutinized and subject to full and open debate. Therefore, they attempt to evade the 'marketplace' and resort to suppressing the expression of others. Thereby, they violate one of our most precious freedoms as Americans.

Why We Should Be Optimistic

Thankfully though, despite this troubling trend, I am actually quite optimistic in a practical sense. I think it is extremely difficult in today's society to shut down expression. With the internet and so many available methods of communication, it's almost impossible to do so.

But I'm even more optimistic because I know that America is a special place. And, as Americans, at our very core, we believe in the right to express ourselves as individuals. We have the freedom to think what we want to think - To say what we want to say - To do we want to do - And to become what we want to become.

So, despite shifting tendencies from time to time, ultimately, as Americans we believe in freedom. Moreover, we understand that freedom of speech is the most vital of our freedoms, and we will do whatever is necessary to protect it.

CHAPTER NINETEEN

BOILING A FROG

Have you ever thought about what it's like to 'boil a frog?' And, interestingly, I mean what it's like from the frog's perspective. May sound like a strange idea, but let me share this story. Perhaps you have heard it before.

Imagine putting a frog into a pot of boiling water. The frog is going to jump out of the pot really fast, right? Now, imagine another scenario where you put a frog in a comfortable, lukewarm pot of water. Over a period of time, you gradually turn up the temperature in the pot one little degree at a time until it reaches a very high temperature, in fact maybe even boiling. The frog never makes the decision to leave. You've boiled the frog.

Why Share This Story?

I see an eerie parallel between the poor frog in a pot of water with gradually increasing temperature and us, the American public.

Now, what do I mean?

In fact, they're on a mission to do as much as they can to, in their view, "improve our lives," meaning pass more laws and issue more regulations. They tell us how to live and they do this day – by day – by day.

As Americans, we live our lives. We work our jobs. Sometimes it's one job. Sometimes it's two jobs. We're taking care of our kids. We're running them off to soccer games and taking them to school. We do whatever's going to be required to really help our kids. We may also be taking care of our parents at the same time. We're just really busy. Come the end of the week -- we're really exhausted.

It also means we can't follow political events day-to-day. We can't fight against the bureaucracy like we might like to in some cases. So, life goes on.

Meanwhile, in Washington (and in some of our states) there's a professional bureaucratic class who have nothing else to do. In fact, they're on a mission to do as much as they can to, in their view, "improve our lives." Meaning pass more laws and issue more regulations. They tell us how to live and they do this day – by day – by day. And, because we are a tolerant people, one more little regulation...and one more...and one more. We may not even be aware of some of them. We say "Okay."

We are living our normal, ordinary, daily lives. Meanwhile, professional bureaucrats are working day-by-day to issue regulations that impact us. In their view, the regulations will improve our lives. In our view, they regulate and restrict our lives; constraining our freedom.

Unfortunately, and generally to our detriment, these bureaucrats are very good at what they do. They're ambitious and they generate many, many regulations. Meanwhile, we don't have the time, the resource or really even the awareness to fight back. So these regulations get promulgated time after time – an endless stream of additional government rules and regulations.

Quantitative Measures

As a quantitative measure, typically there are as many 80,000 pages of new regulations published annually in the United States by our federal government. Now, who can keep track of these? The regulations impact small business. They impact our daily lives and they constrict the ability and freedom of the American people

Interestingly, we were formed as a Republic. As a Republic, we would like our elected representatives to make laws. It may surprise you to find there are only around 400 laws passed in any given year by Congress. Yet, at the same time, each year our bureaucrats generate 80,000 plus pages of regulations. Imagine that?

How can we possibly survive in this morass? Worse yet, many of these regulations make no sense at all.

Here's One for Instance:

This story starts out with what would appear to be a laudable purpose – the conservation of our water resources. On its face, it seems worthwhile objective. A positive concept... So, to put this process into action, the rule makers at the EPA decided that our dishwashers ought to be restricted to 3.1 gallons of water per wash. Sounds good? Actually, not really. Turns out that 3.1 gallons isn't enough water to get the dishes truly clean. The net result – using more water, rather than less - with people washing their dishes twice, directly as a result of the restriction.

There are other crazy instances of regulations shutting down kids' lemonade stands, requiring unnecessary permits, licenses, etc. You know the rest.

How Will We Fight Back?

Well, how is it that we're going to fight against this creeping, incremental bureaucracy? The answer is that it is going to need to be constant, continuing struggle. I know that there are actions being taken now to reduce the burden of regulations – but it will need to be an ongoing and never ending campaign. It is a monstrous, faceless and powerful bureaucracy that we are up against. Some have called it 'The Swamp.' In fact, President Ronald Reagan powerfully described what we are up against.

In referring to the bureaucracy and quoting from C. S. Lewis, Reagan said:

That's the bureaucracy. It moves like clockwork, incrementally taking away our freedoms, one regulation at a time. We as Americans need to stand up and fight this.

This will be a difficult and prolonged struggle – and must include a number of interwoven elements, many of which are difficult to predict in advance.

Thankfully, in general, I do know where the solution lies. It lies back with the story of the boiling frog. If we allow ourselves to get lured into the relaxed comfort of the increasingly warm water – we will boil to death. In our case, the increasingly warm water is the gradually growing bureaucracy with its increasingly burdensome rules and regulations.

Instead of relaxing in the comfort of the warmer and warmer water, we need to think of ourselves as the frog that's being thrown into the boiling water right now. We need to take immediate and decisive action. With the same strength, eagerness and speed, needed by the frog to jump out of the boiling water, we need to rise up and confront the bureaucracy. This is not a fight that we can win incrementally one regulation at a time. Instead, we need to fundamentally change the equation – and once and for all, constrict the power of the bureaucracy to issue a ceaseless series of regulations that constrict our freedoms and limit our lives.

CHAPTER TWENTY

MY VISIT TO CHINA

I was recently in China, visiting Shanghai and Guangzhou. As a first time traveler to China, it was an amazingly eye-opening experience. If you have not been to China, I suspect you would be struck by many of the same observations that impressed me.

Impressions of China

Number one impression: China is massive. And, it is massive in so many ways. I woke up in Shanghai and looked out from my hotel room in amazement. The landscape and skyline was shockingly expansive and far surpassed in sheer height and breadth the skyline of even New York City. An incredible view, made even more impressive when knowing that until quite recently the vast majority of that skyline did not even exist.

The second impression is that it's modern. Oh, my gosh, is it modern. In many of the urban places I visited, say in Guangzhou for instance, these areas truly were pastures and fields thirty years ago. Today there is a really beautiful modern city. Everywhere you look you are surrounded by glass, steel, flowers and greenery. It is well designed and absolutely modern.

Everywhere you look you are surrounded by glass, steel, flowers and greenery. It is well designed and absolutely modern.

I confess this was all a bit surprising to me. Perhaps I was naïve, but I had in mind, maybe the stereotype of the 'Communist Eastern Europe look' - behind the Iron Curtain. I expected it to be gray, drab and just a miserable place to be. China struck me as being quite the opposite.

One more impression: Pride. There's also a certain pride in what has been accomplished. A bit of energy and spark. Elements of entrepreneurism at the local level. Perhaps even a degree of capitalism.

Now it's important to point out, however, that the capitalism does not extend to the larger elements of the economy. While individuals may own and run the local shops, the Party and central planners of the Chinese government are very much in control. This is especially true in the areas of finance, energy, telecommunications and the major infrastructure projects of a planned economy.

Major Takeaway

Beyond the above 'impressions,' my major takeaway, however, is that China is profoundly different from us. China has a different culture and with a very different history and set of experiences than we here in the United States. And, as such, I believe in very significant ways, they will always be different.

At the same time, however, it is quite clear that China is emerging onto the world stage as another superpower, potentially rivaling in some areas the primacy of the United States. As such, China will become an increasingly important player. It is for this reason that it is in our national interest to learn how to deal with China on a cooperative basis even though we recognize there will continue to be major areas of differences as well as areas where we directly compete.

In so doing, we will need to be vigilant. While cooperation will be an important element of our relationship with China, we must never be lulled into complacency. America must stand strong and never relinquish our lead as the dominant military superpower in the world. We cannot allow ourselves to even imagine a scenario where

China's size and increasingly powerful economy lead to military parity with or advantage over that of the United States. This will not be easy. In fact, it will be one of the most important challenges for America in the twenty-first century. However, it is one that we are capable of successfully achieving.

(Note: Despite China's recent progress, I firmly believe that the United States will continue to be the world's primary superpower. I outline this reasoning in the following chapter on 'Competitive Advantage.')

Our formula for American success is clear. We need to focus on reinforcing our core American values. Celebrating and respecting the rights and dignity of the individual, enthusiastically pursuing growth at every juncture and relentlessly protecting our freedoms. Fostering a 'Can Do' spirit here at home while steadfastly defending our national interests from threats from abroad.

If we adhere to these principles in all that we do, including how we deal with China as an emerging superpower, there is no doubt that we will weather all storms and meet the challenges ahead.

CHAPTER TWENTY-ONE

COMPETITIVE ADVANTAGE

This may seem like a fairly dry topic, so let's liven it up a bit and address competitive advantage in the context of the competition between China and the United States.

What is Competitive Advantage?

Essentially, competitive advantage relates to that special and valuable strength or asset you possess, that your opponent does not, which allows you to win. Thus, if you have some critical strength or asset – greater than that of

Many of the same principles that apply to the competition among businesses also apply to the competitive dynamics among nations.

your opponent – and you believe this advantage can be decisive in the struggle, then this is your competitive advantage. And, it is upon this advantage that you must successfully build your game plan or strategy for winning.

Through my own personal experience, I have become very familiar with the topic of competitive advantage. It has been at the core of my business practice throughout my career. First as a Partner at Bain and Company, an international strategy consulting firm, and subsequently in my own firm, The Lucas Group. Interestingly, many of the same principles that apply to the competition among businesses also apply to the competitive dynamics between nations. So, too, China versus the United States.

China's Competitive Advantage

Let's start with facts and trends. When economists make projections, they see very positive trend lines of growth and development for China. Meanwhile, experts typically paint a picture of a stagnating United States, not making significant progress. Then, based on these trend lines, they predict that China will be overtaking us in about thirty years.

A Few Facts about China

- China's population is actually four times that of the United States
- The Chinese economy is growing three times as fast
- There are six cities in China larger than New York City
- There are 15 cities larger than Los Angeles
- Every one of these cities has the advantage of being thoroughly modern in its infrastructure and design because in large part, it has been built during the last thirty years
- The highways, airports and communication systems are sound and right up to date
- It's an exciting, vibrant time to be in China

Danger to the United States

Now, take a moment to really digest the first two points above. Competing with China – a country four times our size, and growing three times as fast! Obviously, it seems inevitable that at some point – unless something changes – we lose, right?

Then, take another moment to look around you and let it sink in a little bit more. Look at the decaying infrastructure in many of our older cities. Pretty depressing. Moving forward, not hard to imagine that we could move into second place or possibly even further down the list from there if things don't change.

Now, take a deep breath and consider the implications. If we fall behind, we as Americans won't have the same opportunities that we do today. Our kids won't. Our economy will obviously suffer.

And, even more important, without the requisite military leadership and strength, we will not have the same ability to live our lives free and protected from threats and dangers from abroad. Our freedoms will be in jeopardy. In fact, our whole way of life. Such a future would be a very dangerous and an almost unimaginable outcome for our great country and thus needs to be avoided at all cost.

However, given the apparent trends described above, what is the answer? What can we do to shape the future in a more positive way? How do we do it? How do we win?

United States Competitive Advantage

Perhaps it should be obvious, but the answer lies in developing a deep understanding of our competitive advantage. We need to identify, focus on and invest in our core strengths that will allow us to win?

What are these core strengths? What is the essence of what will enable us to turn the tables? How can we become the David against this new emerging Goliath?

Thankfully, while the trend lines appear to be against us, we do possess two strong competitive advantages far superior to the Chinese: our entrepreneurial freedom and our entrepreneurial spirit.

- Entrepreneurial Freedom (Based on the Structure of our Economic System)
    - We have a free economy
    - We protect property rights
    - We enforce contract law – predictably
    - We protect intellectual property (very important)
    - We have the free flow of commerce and money throughout our system

- Entrepreneurial Spirit (Based on Personal Freedoms and the American 'Can Do' Philosophy)
    - We honor and celebrate the unique qualities of the individual
    - We protect freedom of speech
    - We protect freedom of religion
    - We protect freedom of association
    - We have virtually unlimited mobility - the ability to move around through our country anywhere we want, anytime we want
    - We have the freedom to choose our jobs – to be anything we want to be

Compare Competitive Advantages

Critically, the freedoms listed above and enjoyed in the United States do not exist to anywhere near the same extent in China. There is no guarantee of freedom of speech, nor freedom of religion. There is very limited freedom to travel. Amazingly, there are very stringent limitations that restrict where you can choose to live in China. In essence, the government makes this decision for you and essentially has the authority to approve or reject any such move you may be contemplating.

Now, this lack of freedom in China was palpably demonstrated to me on a **recent trip to Shanghai and Guangzhou.** On arriving, I did what any typical American might do...I opened up my iPhone. And thought, well, let's see what's going on the world, take a look at Facebook and scroll the news on the internet. From the very get go, I was totally shut down. My access to the free flow of information – the web, social media, etc. – all totally prohibited. The message was clear. In China, it's the government – not the individual who rules supreme.

Now, consider the implications. Take big step back and imagine the implications for China - a country, where the free flow of communication is dramatically curtailed. And, even in those limited ways where you have the ability to communicate, the content of the communication is being thoroughly monitored by the government. Where is the freedom? Imagine the pervasive underlying fear. The deadening impact on the human spirit? The chilling effect on creativity?

With many of the freedoms in China so dramatically curtailed, and in some cases non-existent, it becomes highly uncertain that those ominous trend lines projected by the experts as described above will actually materialize.

While, yes, I know that many predict that China will prevail in overtaking the United States, I do not believe this to be the case. I know that creativity is born of structural economic freedom. It is also given life and vitality through the 'Can Do' spirit of entrepreneurism. In essence, these are our core competitive advantages. And, it is precisely the continued nurturing and application of these core strengths that will enable the United States to maintain economic superiority as well as military and strategic leadership.

Therefore, the recipe and game plan is clear. For the United States to win and for we, as Americans, to continue to enjoy our way of life, we will need to protect, amplify and aggressively invest in our areas of competitive advantage. Specifically, we need to guard and strengthen the structural elements of free our economic system – and we need to celebrate, support and unleash the energy and entrepreneurial spirit of the individual.

With this in mind, it is vitally very important that we protect our freedoms and zealously guard against intrusive and unnecessary government regulation. We know there are some in our government who would like to burden our economy with greater and more restrictive regulation. We know there are also some who would like to greatly constrict our freedom of speech, our freedom of expression, of our religion. We need to do everything we possibly can, at all cost, to make sure it doesn't happen.

Instead, we need to pursue a positive, energetic path where we aggressively invest in accentuating our competitive advantage versus China and the rest of the world. And, in so doing, I have no doubt that we can remain the preeminent nation on the world stage – with the strongest economy and the freest people for generations to come.

CHAPTER TWENTY-TWO

IMMIGRATION

We've been talking a lot about immigration in the last several years. And, despite all the talk and attention, I really don't think the conversation has been framed in the right way. The issue is not really about 'immigration.' Instead, the real issue lies in the difference between 'legal immigration' versus 'illegal immigration.'

So, I would like to start with a fundamental choice:

- Are we going to have a nation of laws?
- Are we going to have an immigration system that's legal, planned, organized and systematic?
- Or are we going to have a system that is chaotic, random, where whoever can get here by whatever means and weave together a life in the shadows is allowed to stay?

I vote for a legal, planned, organized immigration system. A system that is thoughtfully designed and intended to further our objectives as a nation.

True, We Are a Nation of Immigrants

We have all heard the truism repeated many times that in America, "We are a nation of immigrants." And, I think it's a wonderful thing. Hopeful waves of immigrants arriving in America, seeking freedom, opportunity and a better life. Then, assimilating and enriching the fabric of our country.

Everyone's ancestors have come from a variety of places. In my case, I know my ancestors came from Scotland, France, England and Ireland.

As Americans, we represent a rich and diverse set of backgrounds and it is precisely this diversity that makes us stronger. But this is true only to the extent that immigrants assimilate and embrace American values. In other words, while it is true that we are a nation of immigrants, it is far more important that we are a nation of Americans. We are Americans who believe in American values. Core values such as freedom, growth and opportunity.

Immigrants Love Our Freedom

Thankfully, I find that the vast majority of immigrants truly embrace these values as evidenced by my own personal interactions and experiences with those who have recently come to our country. As you may know, I travel a great deal for business and as such, I often find myself in the back of a taxi or an Uber. And, more often than not, the driver has come from another country.

In these situations, I often find myself asking the driver a series of questions, starting with 'Where are you from?' Then asking, 'How long have you been in the United States? And, importantly then following up with "Do you like being here in the United States?" Almost universally, the answer is "I love it here. America is the greatest country in the world"

Then, the ultimate question, "What do you like the most about this country? What's really special about to you about America?" With amazing consistency, nine times out of ten, the answer is always the same. The same one word answer.

And that word is FREEDOM. Freedom is what makes America special. And, this spirit of freedom is a wonderful thing. It is the common bond

...we need to reinvigorate our American values – and generate broad, enthusiastic support as immigrants come to our great nation.

that unites so many immigrants with what they perceive to be the American way of life.

However, for immigration to be successful as a policy, it requires more than simply the perception of an American way of life. It requires several fundamental building blocks.

In sum, a successful immigration policy requires:

(1) the rule of law – immigration based on a predictable and fair set of rules, evenly applied and supported by secure borders;

(2) a clear and thoughtful approach to the question of who gets to come to America, how many, on what criteria, and how answers to these questions benefit America's interests;

(3) a commitment to assimilation – the need for immigrants to assimilate into our culture, adopt our American values and in essence, become Americans;

(4) that we as Americans be receptive to immigrants on this basis; and

(5) that we as Americans never back down from our commitment to preserving our core values of freedom, growth and opportunity while enthusiastically embracing and advancing the 'American Way of Life.'

In other words, on this last point, we need to preserve what makes us special. Unfortunately, this will not be an easy task. Even if we can get clear on a policy – implementing and living these requirements will not be easy. These core American values are under continuous attack. An unhealthy imposition of 'political correctness' has undermined the traditional progression of immigrants toward assimilation – keeping many out of the American mainstream and dividing us as people.

As a result, we need to reinvigorate our American values – and generate broad, enthusiastic support as immigrants come to our great nation. And, it is of critical importance – to do now, as we pass our values on to the next generation.

Threat to Our Freedom

I believe Ronald Reagan got it right on <u>October 27, 1964</u> at the Republican National Convention. His famous speech said,

"Freedom is never more than one generation away from extinction. We didn't pass it to our children in the bloodstream. It must be fought for, protected, and handed on for them to do the same, or one day we will spend our sunset years telling our children and our children's children what it was once like in the United States where men were free."

We have to make sure our children have those same values. And we've got to be teaching it in our schools. We also need to be teaching it in our churches and most importantly in our homes, at the dinner table conversations.

And we need to be inspiring the rich diverse wave of immigrants who come to America to be embracing these same values. If we're going to absorb immigrants going forward and really make this nation stronger, we need to make sure we do a good job of instilling these values. We all want this nation to continue to be the shining beacon of hope in the future just as it has been for many generations past.

In addition to these core values – freedom, growth and opportunity – it's also about the American spirit. The American spirit of hope. It's about optimism. It's about gratitude to be living in the greatest country in the history of the world and the faith in knowing that we have before us the opportunity to achieve even greater success going forward.

CHAPTER TWENTY-THREE

IMPROVING EDUCATION

Improving Education

I've always believed there's nothing more important than a child's education. We have practiced this belief with our own children and have also tried to help other kids, wherever possible, to get a great education.

In our experience, we have found that nearly every child, on the first day of school at the age of five or six, has a great spark. They want to learn. But somehow our educational system often unwittingly conspires against them. And, over time, this wonderful spark may become dimmed or perhaps even extinguished all together.

As such, it we need to start by understanding what it is that causes this to happen – and then design an approach to address it.

Magic Triangle

As a starting point, let's agree on what we call the 'Magic Triangle' of education. The three vital components to achieving success in education with our children. With three parts:

1. **Parents** – Mothers and fathers who really care about his/her own child's education and willing to become actively involved. This is so vitally important and decisive.
2. **Teachers** – Dedicated teachers. The vast majority of teachers get into the profession because they really care about teaching students. Too often, however, bureaucracy, rules and resources get in the way of their efforts.
3. **Students** – Children who come to learn. Consistently supporting them with resources and opportunity so the initial spark does not dim as they get older and go through the school system.

My Friend: Fred Bramante

Back in 1998, when I ran for governor in New Hampshire, Fred was one of the candidates competing with me. He's a really wonderful man and he cares deeply about education. He's trying to revolutionize the way we do education in America.

He tells his own story about not doing well in school. In fact, in his high school class of 212 students, Fred came in at 206th. He tells how his school experience really did have a devastating impact on him. He felt something must be wrong with him. He felt that maybe he was stupid. But over time, he wondered, was it really him, or was it the education system?

After school, Fred started a business. He founded a retail store, which upon the advice of his young children, he named it 'Daddy's Junky Music Store.' It turned out to be a big success. Daddy's Junky Music grew to be the 15th largest chain of music stores in the country.

With his business success, Fred began to really challenge the notion that maybe his lack of success in school wasn't because there was something wrong with him. Maybe there was something wrong with the system. He decided to get involved and as a result eventually became Chairman of the New Hampshire Board of Education. He decided to challenge everything about the system, but in a really positive way.

Most importantly, he came upon a key insight. Fred began to conceptualize that our entire education system is what he referred to as 'time based.' In other words, we go to school for a certain number of days per year, then pass thru a certain number of grades, and then at the end, if we make it all the way thru we have, theoretically, become educated. All of which prompted Fred to ask the question, Should we be really be 'time based,' or would it be more effective if instead, we committed ourselves to being 'learning based?'

Meeting Student Needs

Fred challenged the system with questions like:

- Gym class – if a student is on the gymnastics team and is competing really well, why should we make that student sit through gym class?
- Music class – if a student who is doing really well the in school band or orchestra, why should we expect them to sit through music class?
- Auto mechanics class – if a student is working in a mechanics shop and doing really well, why can't they get credits for their working experience instead of having to sit through shop class?

Stretching this concept even further, he asked the question: why does learning all have to take place by sitting in a structured classroom setting? Why can't students get credits for learning activities that take place outside the classroom?

Giving students the opportunity to learn accounting, law, business, the health related professions – a wide variety of a valuable learnings capable of advancing the student going forward.

While all this seemed to make a great deal of sense, it raised an additional question: If we can be flexible in terms of 'where' the student is learning, i.e. in the classroom versus outside the classroom, could we also be flexible in terms of time? Why a certain number of hours in a school day? 180 days per year? Twelve years of public education? Isn't the fundamental point of education about 'what is learned?' Not about 'how much time is spent?'

Competency Based Education

We all know students learn differently from one another and at different individual rates. So why does everybody have to move along in lockstep fashion as is the typical assembly line process we have in our school system today? Don't we need much more flexibility? Wouldn't it be better if we had a system that would advance students from one level to another based on what and how much they have learned rather than simply how much time they have spent?

These are elements of something Fred has come to call 'competency based learning.' It combines the two elements described above: (1) the flexibility to give students the opportunity to pursue their passions and get credit for learning 'outside the classroom' and (2) to advance and progress thru the system at their own individual rate, as they demonstrate 'competency,' rather than simply spend time, a certain number of hours of attendance.

It's all about competency. As a student moves forward and becomes increasingly competent, he or she moves forward in school. It's about learning. It's not about time. It's not about inflexible rules.

And, I do love the flexibility. Flexibility is so very important in making sure the spark of learning you see in the five-year-old entering school is maintained. It's about giving the student the tools and skills they will need when they become adults. It's about growing and flourishing. It's what our education system really needs to be all about.

I think Fred's initiative toward 'competency based learning' is a terrific idea. It's being embraced all around the country. New Hampshire was the first state to adopt the concept, but it's spreading like wild fire primarily because it makes such wonderful sense.

SECTION FIVE

MAKING A DIFFERENCE
WHERE WE LIVE

CHAPTER TWENTY-FOUR

CHILDREN OF FALLEN
PATRIOTS

Children of Fallen Patriots

Let me tell you about an incredible organization –
Children of Fallen Patriots.   A wonderful cause - with a
focused mission to make sure that every child who loses a
parent in active military service can have a great
education. Fallen Patriots pays for education all the way

through college or vocational school – whatever is going to give that child the opportunity to be all that he or she can be.

Started by a Friend

A friend of mine, David Kim, is a West Point grad who fought in Panama during the struggle against Noriega. While there, tragically a fellow member of his battalion, Sergeant Delaney Gibbs, was killed in combat and left behind an unborn daughter. David wondered what would happen to this little girl and felt a calling to be supportive. One thing led to another, and David along with his wife, Cynthia, founded a fantastic organization. Since then, not only have they helped this one little girl, but Children of Fallen Patriots has also helped more than a thousand other children who have found themselves in a similar situation.

While David is a good friend and the organization was founded many years ago, he had never mentioned the

Children of Fallen Patriots has also helped more than one thousand other children who have found themselves in a similar situation.

effort to me over the years. Then, one day several years ago, he called me and said he thought I might be able to help him in an important way. He said, you have a consulting firm and I hope you can help us figure out something where we don't have an answer. We want to know how many children there are who have lost a parent in active military service. Obviously, this would be important to know for planning purposes and also as a way to get the word out and build support for the organization.

Initially, I thought this would be something easily found in some database or repository of information. But given military privacy laws, such a database does not exist. So, we put a team from The Lucas Group on the issue and began working on it.

What we learned was shocking. Our analysis found that there are nearly 20,000 children in our country who have lost a parent in active military service. This includes loss of life in combat, a training accident, Agent Orange or even suicide. Obviously, from the child's perspective, it doesn't matter. There is a parent who has made the ultimate sacrifice for our country. And, there is a child who deserves our support. We feel, as Americans, we need to take care of those kids. It's an honor and a duty we bear and it is the mission of Children of Fallen Patriots.

My Experience with the Organization

Since being introduced to Children of Fallen Patriots several years ago, I have gotten to know the organization. When you get to meet the mothers, the children and young adults who have now successfully completed school, your heart goes out to them. These are just great, great people. They are great Americans. You can't help but want to get much more deeply involved in what the organization is all about.

Grass Roots Support

Fallen Patriots is such a terrific initiative on so many dimensions. It is about honoring our veterans. It is helping their children. It is all about education. Fallen Patriots is doing all these great things yet there are so many people around the country who are not familiar with the organization or the mission. Many really don't know much of anything about Fallen Patriots. And, how wonderful and important it would be to generate more grass roots support and national visibility?

As one part of such an effort, I suggested an idea and volunteered to help. Why not pick a geography – a state or a region - and go really deep into finding solutions to create that visibility and grass roots support. In other words, by starting with a microcosm to use as a test case or beta site:

- We can create and try a number of different approaches to achieve support and visibility
- We can figure out what works and identify 'best practices'
- And, then develop a 'playbook' based on these 'best practices' that can be applied and 'rolled out' as appropriate from 'state to state' and 'region to region' across the country

As a result, we are doing this in my home state of New Hampshire right now. We're gathering great grassroots support not only to raise money – that's obvious. But one of the other initiatives of real importance is the effort to find or locate the kids. We want to find children who are eligible to receive our benefits.

It may seem as though it would be easy to find them, but it's not. We're developing practices to help us raise money and also help us find children so we can match them with the resources we offer. It's a really important mission.

Moreover, it's so easy to feel good about how the money is being spent. What's really important about an organization like this is the fact that the money ends up directly where it is intended. On average, 98 cents of every dollar raised by Fallen Patriots from third parties actually goes to the education of the kids because board donations cover almost all administration and fund raising costs. In addition, with so many students graduating from college burdened by huge college debt, it's just wonderful to know that the Children of Fallen Patriots has been able to wipe out the entire debt of all those children helped by the program who have graduated college. Now these young adults can go out into the world and be really successful without the worries of repaying heavy financial debt.

Finding the Kids

While it's obvious that there is a need to raise money to support the education of these highly deserving children, it is equally, if not more important, to make sure that we find the children. Of the 20,000 kids in our population who have lost a parent, so far Fallen Patriots been able to identify by name only approximately one-third of those who are eligible. There is such a large number of children yet to be identified.

You may ask why? How could it possibly be true? Part of the answer, as mentioned above, are the challenges imposed by military privacy laws and the absence of an accessible data base. But, in addition, the scenarios that occur in real life can make the task even more complex and difficult.

Let me share one scenario that would not be unusual. Picture this:

- A mother and family living on base
- The get the terrible news the father has died in service
- While they're living on the base, they may have two or three young children
- In a very short period of time, the mother and her children are forced to leave the base and the support system that the base provides – all while trying to deal with enormous emotional stress and financial issues
- Often the young wife will choose to go back to wherever she grew up – which most likely is in some other state, possibly far away – and live with her parents
- She may find a job. May not.
- She may get remarried. May not.
- May move to another place.
- So, as you can see, there are substantial challenges in tracking and finding these deserving kids.

Wonderful Mission

There is no better and more impactful organization than Children of Fallen Patriots. For the children it's about the opportunity for a great education. But, it's also really about being part of a community. A caring organization that is incredibly supportive. Fallen Patriots has such a powerfully positive impact. It literally changes lives.

American Sunshine

CHAPTER TWENTY-FIVE

MILL TOWNS WITHOUT MILLS

As we look across the country, there are so many towns that look so different today than the way they looked twenty to thirty to forty years ago. These were once thriving towns. Today, the people in these towns don't have the jobs they once did. The Main Street's are not bustling with shops and commerce. These towns are not thriving anymore.

In many cases, these towns are essentially 'mill towns without mills.' Or perhaps some other industry has moved away. And, while on one level the enormity of the problem may seem overwhelming, I believe this is an area where we can have a dramatically positive impact.

Let me describe a little bit about my own personal experience, especially in thinking about the before and after. I am vividly aware of this phenomenon and I care deeply about it because in many ways, it describes what has happened to my own home town.

Back in the 1960's and 70's, there were jobs, a main street jam packed with successful local businesses – hardware stores, local pharmacies, clothing stores, jewelers, shoe stores, local

I grew up in Newport, a town of approximately five thousand people, located in the western part of New Hampshire. It was once a thriving town. Yet, today, it's not what it once was. Moreover, the experience in Newport is not really that different from so many other places across the country.

Let me paint the picture. Back in the 1960's and 70's, there were jobs, a main street jam packed with successful local businesses – hardware stores, local pharmacies, clothing stores, jewelers, shoe stores, local grocers, and more. These businesses along with the mills and machine shops provided job opportunities, fueled the local economy and provided vitality and strength to the region. There was an opportunity for young people to grow up in the town and get a great job. There was a strong sense of pride in the community.

Over the last 30-40 years, things have dramatically changed. It's changed in Newport, nearby Claremont and other towns across New Hampshire and across the country. These towns are facing unemployment. The mills are gone. The stores on Main Street are closed. It's hard to maintain the same level of pride.

AND, there's also a major drug crisis.

Opioids are affecting the entire population. Everyone in our town knows somebody who has been directly impacted by this drug crisis.

Turning Around the Decline

Some might say the combination of unemployment, a hollowed out local economy and diminished local pride – all compounded by a ravaging drug crisis – poses an impossible situation. It's too much of a challenge to tackle...we ought to basically give up on these towns. We should provide them subsistence, leave them alone, let them deteriorate. Don't invest.

Obviously, that's not the right answer. We need to turn all this around, but the question is – HOW?

I believe there are things we can do that will make a dramatic difference. It won't be easy – but it is definitely possible. We can take control of our destiny. Here are the three critical things we must do:

1. *Leadership:* Beginning with 'Inspiration and Aspiration,' along the lines we earlier discussed: This can be done, but it's going to take energy and creativity to make it happen. And, importantly, leadership. In other words, we need inspiration, energy and belief saying *"Hey, we're going to do it."* And really mean it. At the same time, we also need the aspiration of an exciting vision and belief saying: *"Not only are we going to do it, but we aspire to create something really great – a bright future."*

2. *Jobs:* To turn a shining vision into reality – it really does require sound economics. We need to bring in good, high paying jobs. Jobs that are consistent with the resources and strengths of each town and region. There is tremendous untapped talent. 'Jobs with a future.' Jobs will fuel the economy and give life support to our towns and cities. Most important, the right kinds of jobs will give young people the opportunity to continue to live, work and raise their families in their own home community. Where they can thrive and grow.

3. Education: We need to work closely with our high schools, vocational schools and local community colleges. We need to give our young people the skills and internships that will allow them to be get plugged into good jobs when they graduate and emerge into the workforce. We need to get away from the notion that everyone needs to earn a college degree – and instead adapt our educational programs to the need for competency and skills that will help all students prepare for a lifetime of success.

4. Cooperation and Coordination: There needs to be a sense of cooperation within the community – linking our educational resources with business and job opportunities. Integrating our schools with the businesses in the community. Providing real life/work experiences to students. And giving businesses the opportunity to shape educational programs to fit the needs of their current and future workforce requirements. Importantly, we need to constantly be 'Thinking Beyond the Region.' In other words, it is easy to become isolated – or 'silo'ed' – in our small local communities – when in reality there are important linkages to jobs and opportunities that can be accessed from other parts of the country or around the world. Either companies that can move into the region or provide jobs or linkages on a remote or virtual basis. The internet really has changed and greatly expanded the way we need to think about the true possibilities available in any specific location.

5. *Pride:* We need to get our pride back. This means community pride – but it also means individual pride. There is a certain pride that comes with self-reliance, with achievement and with earned success. Importantly, this is a pride that snowballs. With each step forward, each accomplishment, it builds and strengthens. It will take some time to develop true momentum – but it will happen, if we can just get the process started.

With pride, local leadership and great jobs, we can create the foundation for solving our current problems and creating positive change. A bright future with hope and optimism are critical components in attacking the drug crisis as well.

Glimmers of Sunshine:

The good news is that we are just now beginning to see signs of progress in Newport, Claremont and other towns around the state.

For instance, a great example of progress already in full swing is Franklin, New Hampshire. Franklin was really down a number of years ago. Thanks to the leadership of Mayor Tony Giunta and his predecessor Ken Merrifield, Franklin is showing real signs of life - aspiration and growth. Much has been accomplished thus far. The main street is starting to come back. The town is welcoming new industry, jobs, housing and more.

We're in the early days. But we are seeing and making progress in towns like Newport, Claremont, Franklin and other communities throughout New Hampshire, New England and across the United States. There's much work to be done. But with the emergence of local pride and aspiration I know we're going to be very successful.

I think there is a powerful vision in reviving and strengthening these great towns and cities across our nation. It is an effort every bit worth fighting for.

I invite you to share this vision as we progress this effort 'town by town' – knowing each town will be unique and different – but there will be important similarities as well. Let's view the Franklin's and Newport's as microcosms – places where we can achieve great success; establish 'best practices' and compile a 'playbook' we can then roll out to other towns and cities across our nation. Lending a critical hand to communities that need help.

Viewing it in this way, imagine the potential. Imagine the positive impact on towns and cities. And, even more so on the lives of so many deserving individuals.. The possibilities are breath taking. The great life and vitality we can bring back to our towns and communities. We are in the early days and the momentum is beginning to build. Acting locally and having a dramatic and positive impact.

CHAPTER TWENTY-SIX

HOPE FOR RECOVERY

The opioid epidemic cuts across all segments of American society. The statistics of addiction and related deaths are horrifying. And, it's not getting any better.

This crisis involves all age groups and all socio-economic classes. It affects everybody. In fact, I suspect you may know someone personally who has dealt with this problem themselves or in their family. Maybe the addiction ended tragically.

Government Involvement

It is clear the government is now aware of the situation. And government agencies are trying to do what they can to confront the situation, or at least address some of the issues. However, government agencies are limited in what they can do. It is

Two Questions:

How can we decrease the demand for opioid drugs?

What can we do about the supply?

difficult to for them to move quickly and they face many restrictions.

Private Efforts

As a result, private, primarily non-profit, non-governmental efforts are critical. They can move more quickly and unburdened by bureaucratic regulations. They can be creative and flexible in their approach.

For instance, in New Hampshire, which is one of the states that has been most severely impacted by the opioid crisis, there is an organization known as 'Hope for Recovery.' It treats substance abuse and recovery in a caring and thoughtful way. The approach is highly personalized, inclusive and meant to focus on the needs of the individual. The founders, Melissa and Andy Crews, have done a tremendous job of developing a model that has the potential to be replicated and shared and thus have a dramatically positive impact on so very many individuals. There is a great need for innovative organizations like Hope for Recovery and other similar models to expand throughout the country.

Two Fundamental Questions

While it's critical to be taking immediate action locally, it's also important to take a step back and think about how we can address the problem on a larger scale and over the longer term. In so doing, there are two obvious and fundamental dimensions to be addressed.

Question One: How can we decrease the *demand* for opioid drugs?

I believe education is critical here. We need to be educating our young people as early as grade school. It should be mandatory and hard hitting.

But, it's not just kids. The opioid crisis has hit adults – and of all ages. I was initially quite surprised to learn one of the fastest growing, and the largest, segments of opioid deaths occurs amongst people in the age group of 45 to 65. Before going down the path of prescription pain medications, we need to provide patients with full knowledge – vivid and explicit – of what dangers lie ahead.

In addition, we need to also address and dampen the demand for opioids and other such substances by doing all we can to provide attractive job and educational opportunities for people, especially those living in some of the hardest hit regions. In other words, opportunities for productive employment and for the chance to get ahead. Opportunities to work hard, earn a living and engage in a busy and healthy lifestyle. My grandmother had a great saying that I don't often hear these days – but seems to apply quite well. She used to say that 'idle time is the devil's playground.' For those who are down on their luck, unemployed and feeling hopeless, these folks are in an especially vulnerable position.

Question Two: What can we do about the *supply*?

We have made some progress in trying to make it much more difficult for physicians to write prescriptions beyond the needs of the actual patient. Both in limiting prescriptions only to those with a true need and limiting the amount prescribed at any given time. However, the guidelines and enforcement continue to be spotty at best.

Meanwhile, the non-prescription, black market sources for opioid drugs need to be forcefully shut down. This will require an increase in the resources for policing and penalizing people who are involved drug trade. Whether the drug is heroin or the incredibly powerful opioid, fentanyl, which is 50 times stronger than heroin, or others, we need to take aggressive action to eliminate the supply. Go the source. Crack down on the distribution. In short, do whatever it takes. .

Obviously, this effort will take a collective resolve. It will also take a substantial amount of money. Here is one creative suggestion. Given the impact of the drug companies in promoting these addictive medications, we can be almost certain that there will be multi-million and probably multi-billion dollar settlements as a result.

Rather than having the preponderance of these funds end up in the pockets of trial lawyers, let's earmark a substantial amount of these moneys to help the true victims and develop solutions. Both programs to shut down supply – such as resources for enforcement – and programs to address demand – generating a bevy of educational initiatives as well as a focus on expanding opportunities for those elements of our population who have been the hardest hit. In other words, let's have the drug companies who have largely contributed to the problem also provide the resources required for addressing the current situation, supporting prevention as well as putting people back on the road to productive lives.

While these combined actions will not be easy, they are representative of the steps we need to take right away to address, and over time, eliminate the opioid crisis in America. It is vitally important we commit ourselves as a nation to taking these actions that will help so very many people lead productive, fulfilling lives and avoid the devastation and suffering that have impacted so many families across our great country.

CHAPTER TWENTY-SEVEN

BUSINESSES THAT MAKE A DIFFERENCE

Traditionally we think about the goals of business as being pretty straight forward. A company is in business to make a profit, take care of its customers and to provide jobs for its employees. These are vital objectives. And, of course, these are going to continue to be foundational and at the

179

core of what it means to be in business for the foreseeable future.

Expanded Business Goals

Today, however, the mission of business is broadening. It is becoming increasingly important for businesses to have a social impact. Business leaders are beginning to think of constituents beyond their employees, their customers and their investors. Beyond making a profit. Businesses are beginning to become aware of and deeply care about the impact they are having on their communities and on the greater world around them.

Everyone wants to feel like, "Hey, I'm in this for more than just making money. Yes, we're going to make sure the bottom line is fine, but I want to do something that is good and to feel like my life and my work have meaning...we really have a purpose here."

On the one hand, these expanded business goals are important and admirable simply on moral grounds. These objectives just seem like the good and right things to do and care about. At the same time, importantly, it turns out that these objectives can also be greatly beneficial as core elements of a successful business strategy.

In other words, there are communities and people outside the company who can benefit from a business in ways that go far beyond the core of the company itself. And in turn, these constituents can be very helpful to the success of the company. In important ways day-to-day, and even more so at critical times when the support of the larger community is required.

Moreover, even within the company, think about the motivation of owners and employees alike. When they go to work every day, they want to be excited. Everyone wants to feel like, "Hey, I'm in this for more than just making money. Yes, we're going to make sure the bottom line is fine, but I want to do something that is good and to feel like my life and my work have meaning...we really have a purpose here." This feeling can be incredibly inspirational. And, of course, can inevitably lead to greater success for the business.

Marula Oil

To make these principles come alive, let me share an example. It's a company called Marula. It is a skincare and hair care company. Its products are based on oil, marula oil, derived from marula trees located in southern Africa.

It's a wonderful product – but it's also a wonderful example of a business that is having a social impact. To produce the product the oil must be extracted by hand from fibers inside the marula fruit. Due to the intricacies of the process and the potential for impurities to seep in, the extraction process cannot be accomplished with machines. Instead, the company employs a workforce of more than a thousand women in the countries of Namibia, Swaziland and Madagascar. All the work is performed by hand.

In return for their labor, the company pays these women cash. On one level, the money is very important as it provides them money to buy food for their families. On another level, it is also very empowering in providing these women a true measure of economic freedom and self-worth, especially as these societies have long been dominated by men. By these practices, Marula is helping to open up new vistas of hope and opportunity for a group of women who historically have been disenfranchised. And even beyond the direct cash payments, the company is also supporting the larger community by providing assistance to the local schools and healthcare programs.

In sum, Marula provides an interesting case example. Like so many other growing companies today, it combines a sound traditional business strategy that is succeeding in the market place while also following through on a social mission and positively impacting lives. It's not difficult to imagine how the social commitment is also helping Marula to achieve business success. Motivated employees coming to work each day, excited to be doing good; while also serving thousands of customers, predominantly women, who are deeply supportive and enthused. Clearly a winning combination!

Unilever

On a larger scale, another company leading in the field of social impact is Unilever. This global giant will be familiar to many as the owner of such brands as Lipton Tea, Dove Soap and Ben & Jerry's Ice Cream. However, the company is now being recognized in ways that transcend its many brands due to its corporate mission: a companywide commitment to sustainability and having a positive impact on all of its constituents. The company, which employs approximately 170,000 people worldwide, has embarked on the 'Unilever Sustainable Living Plan,' focused on generating business growth while both minimizing the company's environmental footprint and increasing its overall social impact.

Main Street

Finally, we don't have to use large companies or brands to see an example of the heightened emphasis on creating positive outcomes beyond the traditional core money making activities of business. Simply go to Main Street or pick a business in your community. Whether they are advertising it or not, chances are that the business may well be engaged in a charitable or social mission, perhaps even right in its own community. Helping the local hospital or contributing to cancer research. Or, simply sponsoring the local Little League team. In fact in one case, I'm aware of one regional printing company that quietly made a commitment to take care of every child of every employee by paying for their college education. Clearly, the combination of all these selfless activities really does make a positive difference.

Wall Street

And beyond Main Street, you can even look at Wall Street. Investors have increasingly come to believe that a company's social mission and activities can also be helpful in making it a more attractive investment. In fact, there are some investors who will only consider investing in companies that are having a positive social impact.

Similarly, some investors have even created rating mechanisms to measure the magnitude of a company's social impact. Then, of course, they can make investment decisions based on those ratings.

Clearly the mission of business is very much expanding. While companies will continue to focus on earning the money they need to sustain themselves, we can all feel good about the expansion of their focus to include a social mission and having a positive impact on people around the world as well as in their very own local communities.

CHAPTER TWENTY-EIGHT

MODERN PATRIOTISM

Patriotism is a term we all know. We think of it in terms like the flag, our troops and the basic freedoms of being an American. It's about our values. It's what we think about on Memorial Day and Veterans Day.

Over time, the term 'patriotism' has also come to mean many different things to many different people. It can be confusing at times.

The differing meaning of patriotism can even create divisions among us. For instance, the recent issue of standing when the national anthem is being played.

Three Basic Elements of Patriotism

I'd like to suggest a concept, a term – that I call 'Modern Patriotism.' It is a unifying and positive idea that I believe can be broadly supported. It builds on our traditional patriotic values and gives each one of us a mission – a way that we can each contribute to our country and to the world.

I hope and believe it is a concept that we can all agree on and help us to march forward together in a very positive way.

To me, Modern Patriotism has three basic elements:

Believing, Achieving and Sharing.

1. ***Believing*** – At the core of believing are our fundamental values as Americans. The most basic and essential of these values is freedom...freedom of speech, freedom of religion, our Bill of Rights and our wonderful freedom to pursue our opportunities as we individually see fit and grow to fulfill our full potential. It is our 'Can Do Spirit' as Americans and our unshakable belief in our nation, what we stand for and our traditional patriotic values.

2. ***Achieving*** – We have an individual opportunity to achieve. At the same time, we also have an individual responsibility to achieve. This means we each need to

do all we can to develop our own capabilities, achieve our own independence as individuals, strive to attain self-reliance and have the opportunity to achieve 'earned success.' Earned success occurs through the hard work and striving required to attain a worthwhile goal. When earned success is achieved it invariably creates enormous satisfaction for the individual who achieves it - which then radiates out to the larger community. Modern Patriotism aspires to the vision that every American be on the pathway to reach his or her own heights of individual achievement and the wonderful self-worth that is enjoyed when success is earned and results achieved. We believe in an America of achievers.

3. **Sharing** – When we have the great joy of being able to achieve, as well as the many tangible benefits that are earned along with it, it is then incumbent upon us to share. We share with others because we want to do good for others and because we are blessed. As Americans, we know that it's the right thing to do. Interestingly, as we share a rather curious thing also happens. The act of sharing actually makes us feel even better about ourselves.

Importantly, as we set out to engage in sharing, we must be very thoughtful. While the simple act of giving can be helpful, the greatest form of sharing is that which empowers others to on go on to achieve their own earned success – after the initial sharing occurs. This is a philosophy of sharing that goes far beyond handouts and is predicated on providing large doses of inspiration, the sharing of a 'Can Do' Positive American

Philosophy and a supportive approach that helps individuals see and pursue the wonderful opportunities that can be achieved. Further, as we engage in sharing with those who are less fortunate, we as Americans can never lose sight of our positive vision and the need to share our optimistic spirit. Sharing much more than simply material support.

So these are the three basic elements. First, believing in the core and founding values of America. Second, achieving – doing all we each can to be all that we can be. And, finally, sharing with others– both here and around the world – inspiring others to pursue their full human potential.

This is Modern Patriotism and when universally embraced can form the basis of a very bright future for all of us here in America and the world.

AFTERWORD

Wonderful Example: Modern Patriotism by American Newcomers

Modern Patriotism embodies the essence of what it is to be an American. It is at the core of our fundamental values. While we can embrace these principles in concept, there will inevitably be challenges as we attempt to put them into practice.

In fact, often we may find it is easier to slip into thinking why something can't be done – rather than why it can. For some, that may well be true of Modern Patriotism. However, it's really not that difficult to put Modern Patriotism into action if we start with a 'Can Do' optimistic spirit.

To illustrate, let me share an example. It highlights how one group – totally new to America -- is overcoming these challenges – and by contrast can serve to inspire many of us who have grown up in America and faced with lesser challenges, to rise to the occasion.

I have gotten to know a community in America who comprise the Diaspora from South Sudan. Located in a land-locked region of eastern Africa, South Sudan is a very, very poor country and has gone through years, actually decades, of civil war. Many of the people who were able

They are living their lives and practicing the values of Modern Patriotism. We need only to believe, to achieve and to share.

189

to escape have moved to the United States.

I have great respect for this community. They are living examples of those who believe, achieve and share. They've come here to the United States and they love our country. They are putting Modern Patriotism into practice.

They 'believe' in our fundamental values. They are so thrilled to be here in America and are working to be everything they possibly can be.

They 'achieve.' Despite limited resources, they are doing all they can to work hard, educate their children, learn our language and fit into our society. They do this while also maintaining their own culture.

They 'share' amongst their community. They are getting ahead here in the United States, but they are passionate about sharing with their brothers and sisters back in South Sudan. It's vitally important because in South Sudan, more than ninety percent of the people have to exist on less than one dollar per day. The sharing and generosity of the South Sudanese living in America is absolutely critical to the people of South Sudan today and will contribute mightily to the future of this new country.

The South Sudanese are just one example. There are many other instances throughout our land of people who have recently arrived in America and who believe in our values. These are people and communities who are achieving and sharing. They are living their lives and practicing the values of Modern Patriotism. We need only to believe, to achieve and to share.

ABOUT THE AUTHOR

Jay Lucas serves as Chairman and Managing Partner of The Lucas Group, a strategy consulting firm that he founded in 1991, focused on the specialized needs of private equity investors and their portfolio companies.

Previously, Jay served as Vice President and Partner of Bain & Company and during his career has helped numerous executives, investors and management teams set their strategic direction and grow their businesses.

In addition, Jay is the Founder and Managing Partner of Lucas Brand Equity, a fund that invests in small growing brands in the beauty sector – skincare, haircare and cosmetics – then applies expertise to help them grow and create value. Lucas Brand Equity currently has investments in portfolio brands sourced from around the world and marketed in major retail channels throughout the United States and abroad.

In addition to his business activities, Jay has been actively involved in politics and government, serving two terms as a member of the New Hampshire House of Representatives where he was a member of the House Judiciary Committee. In 1998, Jay ran for Governor, winning the Republican primary and then serving as his party's nominee in the general election.

He is a strong supporter of our veterans, leading the effort in New Hampshire for 'Children of Fallen Patriots' – an organization devoted to making sure that every child who loses a parent in active military service can have their education paid for all the way through college. Thus far, Fallen Patriots has helped more than one thousand surviving military children pay for their education.

Jay earned his MBA from Harvard Business School and his J.D. from Harvard Law School. He earned his undergraduate degree from Yale University and attended Oxford University as a Marshall Scholar where he studied International Relations and Military History.

Looking Toward the Future with 'Can Do' Optimism and
Positive Spirit!

Made in the USA
Middletown, DE
12 September 2022